Faces in the Crowd

Chris Beckett

FACES
IN THE CROWD

A JOURNEY IN HOPE

CHRIS BALE

THE CHINESE UNIVERSITY PRESS

ISBN: 962-201-885-8

THE CHINESE UNIVERSITY PRESS
The Chinese University of Hong Kong
Sha Tin, N.T., Hong Kong
Fax: +852 2603 6692, 2603 7355
E-mail: cup@cuhk.edu.hk
Website: http://www.cuhk.edu.hk/cupress/w1.htm

Printed in Hong Kong

Contents

For Rowan, Hayley, Catherine,
Lorna, Jennifer, Beth, David,
Ruth and Peter, whose journeys
are just beginning.

Introduction

Faces in the Crowd

A mother outside a hospital in the Philippines, cradling a baby in her arms. A sugar cane labourer, also in the Philippines, sitting on the floor of his hut one night and speaking simply and quietly of his hopes for his children. A young man in Hong Kong trying to come to terms with the trauma of losing both his legs after a road accident. A student in Bangkok, dreaming of life beyond the city's most notorious slum. A young mother in a poor village in West Bengal, struggling to raise a family. An English banker giving up a promising career to help children on the streets of Calcutta. A little boy in Pakistan, suffering from leprosy.

Faces encountered during twenty years of living and working in Asia and travelling as director of a development agency, Oxfam Hong Kong. There were so many faces, of course — hundreds, even thousands of them. Yet these few were special, once seen and never forgotten, people whose stories and situations touched me deeply.

Sometimes, years later, there were fleeting thoughts — 'I wonder what happened to...' But of course there was no way of finding out. Life had moved on. I hadn't seen or heard of any of these people for many years, didn't know where they were, didn't even know if they were still alive. Families would surely have moved, slums been cleared, hospital records lost. It would be impossible to find them after such a long time.

Or would it?

I decided to go back. Back to the same slums, the same plantations and the same hospitals, looking for the same people, to see how their lives had changed.

This is the story of that search, a journey which started in a fishing village on the shores of an island in the central Philippines and ended seven months later on the hot, dusty streets of Karachi.

A journey in hope.

A Journey in Hope

CHAPTER 1

Philippines, Negros Occidental
Punta Taytay

Leilani Flores

1986 — War and Famine

The last time I was in Negros Occidental there was a war going on.

Well, not a war in the pitched battle and heavy artillery sense of the word, more a series of scraps between government troops and guerillas of the Communist New People's Army. In one confrontation, the rebels came down from the mountains and ransacked a town, killing twenty-five people. Two police stations were attacked and the army, bent on revenge, raided villages to 'flush out insurgents'. I sat in the passenger terminal at the airport and watched rockets being loaded onto military helicopters.

Yet the provincial capital, Bacolod, hemmed in by road-blocks and an overnight curfew, seemed such an unlikely venue for a war, being a pleasant, relaxed, coastal city, fanned by gentle sea breezes. People went about their lives as usual, smiling and laughing, and the armoured vehicles which trundled around the city's plaza at sunset looked ludicrously out of place, like a herd of elephants marauding through a suburban garden. Only the fighters and their victims seemed to take the war seriously.

I was drawn to Negros not by the fighting but by reports of famine and, in particular, by the insistence of an Oxfam colleague that I should go to see the province's children. He had been there and said simply, 'You won't believe your eyes.'

Negros is one of the largest of the Philippines' seven thousand islands, lying in the central Visayas region, a fifty-minute flight southeast from Manila. For almost two centuries, it has been the country's main sugar producing region and the *haciendas* or plantations still stretch away to distant horizons. The wealth and health of two and a half million people depend on the vagaries of the international sugar market, and when in 1985 the price of sugar plummeted and many plantation owners stopped or drastically reduced production, the effect on poor people was devastating, far worse and much more wide-

spread than any hardships caused by the fighting. Families in the urban slums saw their incomes fall as the island plunged into recession, and sugar workers out on the plantations found themselves without any work at all. Families simply could not afford to eat. Many babies and young children died.

The children's wards at Bacolod hospital became so full that some patients died on wooden benches in the lobby. I visited the hospital a number of times in 1986 and 1987, took many photos, asked many questions, said many prayers. I remember the humiliation of standing alone in the middle of a ward, surrounded by dying children, and realizing that I

6

couldn't do anything to help them. I had never felt so completely and utterly useless.

Of all the hundreds of children who passed through the hospital in those terrible years, one little girl in particular stuck in my mind. She was the first child I met on the first day of my first trip to Negros, and I recorded our meeting in my diary.

September 15, 1986

First stop, the paediatric department at the provincial hospital in Bacolod. I was in good spirits, eager to learn. It seemed safe to assume that the suffering here would not compare with what I saw in Ethiopia and Sudan in early 1985.

But on the steps of the hospital I met a mother holding her baby, a girl of eleven months called Leilani Flores. Leilani had spent nine of her eleven months in the hospital's malnutrition ward. She had made some progress and her mother was taking her home.

I looked down at her and felt the same shiver of fear that I had experienced in Ethiopia. The staring eyes, the wrinkled skin, the pathetically thin arms — those familiar signs. Surely it was not happening again, not here.

It was happening again, there in Negros, where the climate is perfect and the soil is rich and fertile. Leilani was a casualty of a man-made disaster.

Strange, really, that I should remember this one child whom I met for no more than a couple of minutes on the hospital steps. Other children's faces faded from memory, but I couldn't forget the moment when Mrs. Flores unwrapped the sheets she was cradling in her arms and showed me her daughter — such a tiny, shrivelled little baby, so very vulnerable. Perhaps I remembered her because she frightened me so.

7

When I was next in Negros a few months later I checked on Leilani's progress and she was doing well, back up to seventy-five per cent of the proper weight for her height, but that was the last I heard of her.

So in 1997, eleven years after that first meeting on the hospital steps, I went back to Bacolod to try to find her.

Happy Endings

The first thing that struck me was that the intervening years had been pretty good for Bacolod.

The rebel fighters had retreated into the mountains to lick their wounds and the soldiers were back in barracks. The price of sugar had been fairly stable and so peace had been accompanied by a good measure of prosperity. Bacolod had acquired the emblems of urban middle-class life — a drive-thru McDonalds, shopping malls, mobile telephones and even its own cable TV station. The young professionals in their designer sunglasses

were brand-conscious and every teenaged boy wanted a Chicago Bulls vest or a Michael Jordan cap. Of course, some people still struggled to keep body and soul together but for most of its residents Bacolod was clearly a more comfortable and more affluent place than it had been a decade before.

The Sea Breeze Hotel, though, had seen better days. At least, I hope it had. It had been built forty years earlier and appeared not to have been cleaned or decorated since. The bed sheets had the stains and smells of too many long nights, and one morning when I turned on the tap the pressure of water spat the entire shower fitting at me. Waves had once lapped at the hotel's foundations but now broke half a mile away across a vast overgrown area of reclaimed land, so that instead of facing the sea my room opened straight into the dark upper branches of a fig tree. Most of the staff looked as though they had been there since the doors first opened, but they were very friendly and as the days went by I began to rather enjoy the lazy, faded air of the place.

Every time I stepped outside I was greeted like a pop star or a sporting hero, with people waving and calling out, 'Hey, *tiyo* Romano!' Before celebrity status could turn my head, I discovered that *tiyo* or uncle Romano was a benevolent old man in a television commercial for engine oil. Couldn't see the likeness myself. Or wouldn't.

The search for Leilani Flores began with a flick through the Bacolod telephone directory, looking for the names of doctors whom I had met at the hospital a decade before. Sure enough, one of them was there. Dan Duenas. A small man with a round face and a ready smile.

'Dan, it's Chris Bale. I don't know if you remember, but ten years ago...'

'Sure, I remember.'

Dan was running his own private paediatric practice. It was, he said, a different world from those nightmare days at the hospital.

'If you are in private practice, you get to see mostly well patients,' he said. 'Because these people can afford to pay, they come to you with very little things. Most of the time, I just don't see those really serious cases.'

We had dinner together and recalled the days when every case had been serious, when Dan and the other doctors had battled through twenty-four-hour shifts and been surprised if they

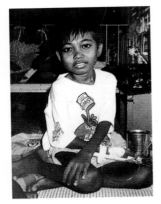

saw the sun rise without having lost at least one child. The hospital had been so short of resources in those days that the doctors had had to dip into their own pockets to pay for drugs, blood and medical tests. Oxfam had stepped in with a monthly grant, a small response to a large tragedy but one which saved lives. A cheque book was no match for the skills of a surgeon or the dedication of a nurse but it had its uses.

'I'm trying to find a girl you treated back in 1986,' I said to Dan.

He leaned back in his chair and frowned.

'I don't know if I can remember,' he said. 'It's a long time ago. I left the hospital in 1989, you know.' A pause. 'There were so many children.'

'Well, her name is Leilani Flores. I met her...'

'Oh, yes, I do remember that child,' he said quickly with a grin. 'After I left the hospital, I helped a fishermen's organization and one day I went to a fishing community just south of Bacolod. Mrs. Flores was there and she called out to me, 'Doctor, doctor, do you remember my child? We had no medicines and you were the one who helped us.' Actually, I didn't remember her, but I just said that it wasn't me who helped her, it was the Oxfam fund. You know, Chris, that fund helped so many patients.'

'Do you remember the name of the place?'

'Punta Taytay. I'll drive you there after dinner, if you like, so that you'll know where to look for her.'

We climbed into Dan's ancient Volkswagen Beetle, its bodywork blood red and battle scarred. The air-conditioning system seemed to be linked directly to the petrol tank and the windows were covered with a black plastic film which was designed to reduce glare but actually cut visibility to a few feet. We lurched forward into the night and, after taking a wrong turn off the highway, began to bump along rough, unlit roads, with the engine making enough noise to waken the dead. We turned left, turned right and were soon lost, but then, chugging along a dark and deserted lane, the old car's headlights lit up a sign saying Lovera's Store.

'It's here,' said Dan, stopping the car. 'When you come back, just walk past the store towards the beach over there and the Flores's house is on the first corner. It's quite easy to find.'

I peered into the night, trying to memorize the store, looking for other landmarks.

'There are many people here called Flores, so when you check the girl's medical records at the hospital ask for the father's first name and the mother's first name, so that you can be sure.'

I suddenly recalled a trip that Dan and I had made ten years earlier — in another battered old car, to another poor seaside community.

We had been searching that time for a little boy called Rommel Benedicto, who had spent months in the hospital's intensive care unit suffering from severe malnutrition, pneumonia, measles, typhoid and congestive heart failure. For six weeks he had been in a coma, but then, to the doctors' amazement and delight, he had recovered and been sent home. Dan had called him 'the boy who came back to life from death.'

My diary from that day back in 1987 read:

Late in the afternoon we drove out to Rommel's village on the outskirts of Bacolod. The Benedicto family's hut was beside the sea and as we stepped inside, a crowd of giggling, curious children gathered around us.

Dr. Duenas explained why we had come. Mrs. Benedicto went into another room and returned carrying a chubby little

boy in a white vest — Rommel.

In the last of the afternoon sunshine we went out onto the sand with all the children and I took one last picture, just to show that Negros is not all about suffering and sadness. People smile and children play, and some stories have happy endings.

But Leilani Flores. Of her, I had no pictures. Only a memory — and the hope that her story too would have a happy ending.

The Boy with No Name

I returned to the regional hospital with some trepidation. Ten years earlier I had at least had the comfort of knowing that Oxfam's grant was easing some of the pain of some of the children, but this time there would be no shield from the suffering. I arrived with a notebook not a chequebook, questions not answers.

Doctora Cecilia Labra, one of Dan Duenas's young colleagues a decade before, had stayed on at the hospital and become Head of the Paediatrics Department. She introduced me to her team, including the senior resident Doctora Ceres Baldevia-Gay, a bright, vivacious woman, toughened by dealing with the dark side of life but not yet jaded by a surfeit of death.

Four young trainee doctors wanted to see the photographs of children I had met ten years earlier, but when I showed them the pictures they recoiled in horror, clearly not accustomed to seeing such horribly emaciated patients.

'No,' said Dra. Labra, 'we don't get to see the very seriously malnourished children that I used to see here. We still have one once in a while, but it's not so common.'

Statistics confirmed the improvement. The number of children admitted to the hospital each month had hardly changed over the past decade but the number of deaths had been halved. Plain proof of progress.

However, this was a government hospital with most of the children coming from poor families, and the combined effects of poverty and lack of education meant that many still died unnecessarily. More than half of the children were below the proper weight for their height and parents often waited until their child was at death's door before bringing him or her to the hospital. More than half of the children who died did so within twenty-four hours of admission.

'You take one look at them and you know you can't do anything,' said consultant Dr. Benito Bionat. 'Just call the priest.'

'But when the patient arrives you give them everything,' added Dra. Baldevia-Gay quickly. 'You go out of your way to help them. You treat them as one of your relatives and you really get to know them and their families. Even though you

13

know there is no chance any more, you still have to do every-thing.'

'It must be very demoralizing for you,' I suggested, 'to see children dying just because they arrive here too late.'

'At your first death you cry,' said Dr. Bionat. 'Later you learn to develop a wooden heart.'

Stacked in a corner of the doctors' common room were the old registers containing the details of every child ever admitted. Somewhere in that vast lexicon of names and diseases would be a record of Leilani, but before starting to search for it I joined the doctoras on a round of the wards.

We stopped first beside a cot in the intensive care unit, in which a baby girl was hooked up to a tangle of tubes and machines. Her young parents from a fishing village along the coast were looking down on their newborn daughter — such a tiny little life, surrounded and sustained by technology. Her name was Joselle Escasulatan and she had been born with a cyst on her left lung, which had caused her heart to move, which in turn had prevented her right lung from functioning properly. The abnormality had been spotted before birth on an ultrasound scan, she had been operated on and the doctoras

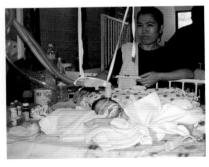

hoped she would make a complete re-covery.

'The last time you were here,' said Dra. Labra, 'we didn't have ultrasound, we didn't have a consultant, we didn't have an intensive care unit, we didn't have a ventilator, we didn't have the same post-operative care. This child would certainly have died.'

More plain proof of progress.

But it is in the nature of hospitals that happiness and sadness are never more than a cot apart, and a few minutes later we paused beside an eight-day-old baby boy who was lying on a bench in the hospital lobby. He had been admitted the previous evening and I asked Dra. Labra for the prognosis.

'Very bad,' she said. 'I don't know if he can survive another twenty-four hours. He was born at home in the mountains with a traditional birth attendant who cut the umbilical cord with a bamboo stick. He's had breathing difficulties with secretions into his lungs and now the infection has spread to the blood — and he has pneumonia. The trouble is that the parents waited eight days before bringing him here.'

The baby needed help with breathing but the hospital's two ventilators were already being used for other children, so his father and uncle were taking turns to pump oxygen to him manually. His mother, who had suffered measles three days before giving birth, now had pneumonia but was refusing to go to the outpatients' department for treatment because she couldn't afford to pay for medicine. Instead, she sat at the end of her baby's bed with a rasping cough, her face drained of all emotion.

Dra. Labra explained to the parents that the outlook for their son was very bad. They asked if they could go home because nothing more could be done, but she insisted that they stay, promising that everyone would do their best to save the boy's life. When they protested that they couldn't afford to pay for medicines, she quietly assured them that from now on everything would be free of charge.

'What is the baby's name?' I asked.

Dra. Labra spoke to the parents in their Ilonggo dialect and then turned back to me.

'No name,' she said.

We walked on. The respiratory ward was almost empty ahead of the rainy season and there were only a few children in the isolation ward. In the gastro ward, Dra. Baldevia-Gay pleaded with a young woman and her husband to allow doctors to operate on their newborn daughter, saying the girl urgently needed surgery to correct a serious intestinal problem. Finally, she turned away, exasperated.

'They just say they will leave it to God,' she said. 'These people!'

A few minutes later the doctora had a problem of a different kind. Money.

Two weeks earlier, Chochie Padronia's mother had searched high and low for a box of matches. Unable to find any at home, she had popped out to buy some, leaving eleven-month-old Chochie and his four-year-old brother at home. In fact, Chochie's brother had hidden the missing matches and while his mother was out he played with them. A fire started, the family home was destroyed and Chochie was terribly burned. He lay in the intensive care unit, drifting in and out of

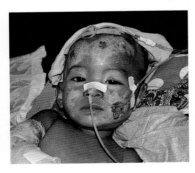

consciousness, and the doctora was due to fly with him that afternoon to a specialist burns unit in Manila. Then, barely four hours before the plane was to take off, a donor who had been expected to pay for Chochie's grandmother to stay with him in Manila decided not to help, and so instead of caring for sick children the doctora was rushing around asking for donations. The search for money would take time and so Chochie would be staying in Bacolod for a few more days.

'Will that jeopardize his recovery?' I asked.

'Not really,' said Dra. Baldevia-Gay, 'but in Manila they have specialist facilities and they can control any infections better.'

As she spoke, a cat walked slowly across the lobby and into one of the wards.

We returned to the doctors' room and I began to search through the old hand-written registers of admissions and discharges. Some of the new trainee doctors wanted to help and so we all sat around a large table, running our fingers down the columns of names.

Finally, I found a first entry for Leilani Flores.

Name	Lailanie Flores
Admitted	April 7, 1986
Age	Six months
Home	Bacolod City
Father's Occupation	Orchid Vendor
Diagnosis	Bronchopneumonia
Admitted by	Dr. Socorro Gonzaga
Weight at admission	2.4 kgs
Date of discharge	June 16, 1986
Weight at discharge	4 kgs

The spelling of Leilani was different but there seemed little doubt that this was the right child. I had seen her at the hospital in September 1986, so presumably she had been readmitted.

Dan Duenas had advised me to check her parents' first names but this entry didn't show them. Perhaps the next one would.

A nurse came in and called Dra. Baldevia-Gay away but the trainee doctors and I continued searching through the registers, page after faded page. Eventually, another brief note. On June 25, 1986, just nine days after being discharged, Leilani had been re-admitted with 'acute viral syndrome'. This time her parents' first names were shown — father Rodrigo and mother Erlinda.

As I was closing the register, Dra. Baldevia-Gay slipped quietly back into the room.

'You know the boy in the lobby with the oxygen pump?' she said.

I nodded.

'He just died.'

The boy with no name. Dead after just eight days. In another time and another place, he could certainly have been saved, but there and then in Negros he was just one more tiny victim.

The boy's parents faced one final sordid complication — how to get the body of their son back to the mountain town of Don Salvador Benedicto for burial. An undertaker would be prohibitively expensive, so the journey would have to be by public transport.

'But,' said Dra. Baldevia-Gay, 'the buses won't let them travel with a dead body because it's bad luck. So we tell them to put the body in a small box before they get on the bus.'

She smiled sadly. 'And try not to cry on the journey.'

The Calachuchi Tree

The night before we set out to find Leilani, I lay awake listening to torrential rain pounding the leaves of the old fig tree outside my window. The long dry days were over and it seemed the rainy season had begun. The storm buffeted the window for hours and by first light a large puddle of water had formed on the floor of my room. Then, on a tropical impulse, the skies suddenly cleared and we walked out into a fresh morning, along streets washed of the summer's dust.

Through the Governor's Office, I had recruited a companion to help with translation between Ilonggo and English. Emmanuel Arenas, known to one and all as Amik, was twenty-five years old. He was studying computers but only because his mother had diverted him from his original goal of becoming a policeman. We were a good match — Amik could help me with translation and my search gave him a chance to do some detective work.

He had already discovered that the electoral records office had no listing for Rodrigo and Erlinda Flores at Punta Taytay. However, the newly elected *barangay* captain or neighbourhood council chairman was a Mrs. Leonila Flores who, we were told, might well be related to Leilani's parents.

So, carrying a large tin of biscuits as a gift for the family, we boarded an old blue jeepney and within half an hour arrived at Punta Taytay. It was a Sunday and the little seashore community was already being overrun by people from Bacolod who had come out from the city to spend a day on the beach.

We soon found Lovera's Store, but Dan Duenas's instructions, which a few nights earlier had seemed so clear, now made no sense at all. We couldn't 'walk past the store towards the beach and find the Flores's house on the first corner' because a barrier blocked the way to the seashore and there were no houses to be seen.

Mrs. Flores, the *barangay* captain, was in her office a little further down the road, a plump, smiling woman in a red floral print dress. Amik asked for the address of Leilani's father, Rodrigo, but Mrs. Flores said she wasn't sure and suggested that we walk back the way we had come and try to find a man called Marcelino Flores, who lived opposite the school.

'So,' I said to Amik as we retraced our steps, 'we are going to see Marcelino Flores, who is the brother of Leilani's father. Right?'

'Alleged,' said Amik, with a detective's professional caution. 'Not yet proven.'

Back at Lovera's Store, half a dozen people were already sheltering from the soaring sun, and when Amik mentioned to them that we were looking for Rodrigo and Erlinda Flores, a woman with protruding teeth stepped forward.

'I am Rodrigo's sister,' she said.

Amik explained that we were actually trying to find Rodrigo's daughter, Leilani.

'Meilanie,' corrected the woman, smiling at me and adding in English, 'But she is not here. She is in Tagum in Davao del Norte.'

20

That was not good news, for Davao del Norte was hundreds of miles away on the island of Mindanao. However, before contemplating a long voyage south, I wanted to check why the woman had changed Leilani's name to Meilanie.

'How old is Meilanie?' I asked.

'About twenty-five, I think.'

'No, that must be another daughter. We are looking for Leilani. She is eleven.'

The woman looked puzzled and repeated the name a couple of times.

'Leilani... Leilani.'

Then, a flash of recognition.

'The malnourished?'

I nodded.

'Dead already.'

I sighed. 'Oh, no.'

It was so stark and final, so utterly hopeless. 'Dead already.' Over the previous few days I had begun to picture Leilani as a happy, healthy eleven-year-old but now suddenly those dreams were smashed. The little shrivelled baby whom I had met on the hospital steps had lost her struggle for life. There was to be no happy ending.

'When did she die?'

'Oh, a long time ago.'

The woman, whose name was Merlyna Flores, remembered that her niece had come home to Punta Taytay after months in hospital. She had seemed to be winning her long battle against malnutrition and had been baptized. Then suddenly she had fallen ill and died of 'fever'.

'How old was she then?'

'I don't know. Maybe about two years old. All the other

21

children were healthy, but she was very small and her complexion was very pale. Her skin was white. She was very sick.'

A small crowd was gathering and one of Leilani's cousins said he remembered playing with her. He recalled a happy baby. 'Always smile but sometimes cry because no food,' he said. Yet it was obvious that Leilani's relatives were not really recalling a niece or a cousin — merely a sick child long gone. In this country teeming with children, Leilani Flores had just been one who didn't make it.

Rodrigo and Erlinda had stayed on at Punta Taytay for a time with their other children, but after a few years they had moved to Tagum, where Rodrigo was still selling orchids. The hut in which they had lived, right where Dan Duenas had remembered it, had been demolished.

There seemed little point in us staying in Punta Taytay, but the day was young and Merlyna wanted us to meet one of her brothers, so we walked up the

road to where Marcelino Flores had set up a new bamboo stall, hoping to sell native cakes and soft drinks. The stall was directly opposite the front gates of Punta Taytay Elementary School and Marcelino was sure that when classes resumed in two weeks' time his business would boom. Today, though, things were very slow. People from the city were streaming past the stall on their way to the beach but so far nobody had stopped to buy anything.

So while Marcelino waited for his first customer, we sat and talked about life in Punta Taytay.

Merlyna explained that her husband had left her years

ago and that she was bringing up two sons on her own — fourteen-year-old Kevin and seven-year-old Kenneth. Kenneth, in a frayed white T-shirt, was very small for his age. Kevin, tall and slim, was the three-pointer for the Midgets basketball team. He wanted to be an engineer but was falling behind with his education — at fourteen he should have completed his first year in high school but actually still had two years to complete at elementary school, having dropped out from time to time when his mother didn't have enough money to pay his fees.

Merlyna explained that she scrambled together a few *pesos* from various sources. Sometimes she did laundry for rich neighbours and today she had been to early Mass at five o'clock in the morning in order to be free to work a full day serving at Lovera's Store, for which she would be paid 40 *pesos*, about one US dollar.

She led us through a coconut grove to a collection of dilapidated huts and walked up to one of them.

'Welcome to my humble home,' she said with a smile.

The hut was literally falling apart. There were gaping holes in the roof, with sheets of plastic suspended hopefully on the inside in a vain attempt to catch the worst of the water. During the previous night's downpour, the family had been soaked and unable to sleep. There was a small living area, beyond which were two even smaller bedrooms. Amik peered into the living area and, uncertain what to call it, said, 'Ah, the *sala*.'

Merlyna burst out laughing at such a grandiose term.

'The receiving room! It's more like the servants' quarters,' she said.

An electric light hung from the ceiling but the power had been cut years ago because Merlyna couldn't pay her bills. The hut had no kitchen and so she cooked outside. There was a communal toilet and water came from a well. Merlyna was a squatter and, like all her neighbours, could be evicted from the land at any time, so although she owned her hut, it wasn't exactly a prime piece of real estate. Frankly, it was barely enough for a decent bonfire.

Sitting in the doorway was the matriarch of the Flores family, eighty-six-year-old Jovita, who had been born in Punta Taytay and had never moved away. She was very frail and unable to stand without support.

I wondered whether she remembered Leilani.

'Who?' she asked.

How many grandchildren did she have?

She had no idea, but Merlyna and Marcelino made a quick calculation.

'Well, Rodrigo has five and Marcelino has seven. Pacifico has six and another brother has eight. Merlyna only has two but another sister has plenty.' They concluded that the total was 'about thirty-five.'

Amik smiled. 'The trouble with this family,' he said, 'is that they keep... '

'Expanding?' I suggested.

'Every night!'

Merlyna needed to return to work at the store and so we made our way back out to the road. As we walked, she turned to me and said quietly, 'I am not ashamed of my situation.'

I admired her dignity. Merlyna realized that her home was a hovel, that Kevin was already behind with his schooling and that Kenneth would probably fare no better, and she was of sufficient years to know that she would probably see out her days there, in poverty on the western shores of Negros. Maybe others would have lived this life differently and some might criticize her, but I respected her deeply. Deserted by her husband and gripped by poverty, she was doing the best she could for her boys.

We walked slowly back to the stall, surrounded by children. One of them called out, 'Hey, *tiyo* Romano!' and they all convulsed in giggles. Marcelino's eldest son Harold slipped quietly into the group. He was fifteen, very small for his age and had long wavy hair. At first, he just looked at me steadily and smiled, saying nothing, like a firework waiting for a spark, but within a few minutes he burst into life and became the family spokesman.

Harold had dropped out of school a year earlier and was unlikely to return. Instead, his days were spent helping the fishermen or grubbing about on the beach for shellfish such as *talaba* and *si-si* to sell in the market. His father praised Harold's maturity and sense of responsibility, but to me he seemed very young, a small boy expected to live a man's life.

Harold and cousin Kevin led us down to the beach, a stretch of greyish brown sand, dotted with the flotsam and jetsam of many tides. Hundreds of people were playing in the sea or eating snacks in thatched shelters under the palm trees, but the cousins ignored the bathers and walked across to where the fishing boats were beached.

Harold said it would cost 30,000 *pesos* or 750 US dollars to buy a medium-sized boat, an almost impossible dream for him and his family, but even without his own boat the boy was well

versed in the ways of the sea. He explained how the boats were launched and pointed towards the horizon to indicate the best fishing grounds. His small fingers expertly untangled a net which had been hurriedly stowed on deck. Sometimes, he said, instead of paying money for his labour, the fishermen paid him in fish, which he either sold in the market or took home for the family to eat.

We turned and walked back along the beach and I observed the two cousins. Kevin, dressed in his basketball strip, was quiet and serious, watching me warily, trying to make sense of this stranger who had walked unexpectedly into his family's life. Harold, by contrast, was having fun, posing for photographs, amusing Amik and me with the way in which he mixed English and Ilonggo. He had tied a piece of black string around his left wrist so that he could pretend he was wearing a

watch and told us that he dreamed of becoming a pop singer. The shy one and the showman, teenaged types found the world over. These two were materially very poor but they were also wonderfully secure in their environment. Sure of their family,

sure of the seasons, sure of the sea.

I thought again of Leilani, the boys' dead cousin, and realized that it was time to move on. Too many tides had rolled to shore. The way to respect the dead was to respect the living.

I looked at my watch and saw that it was lunchtime.

'Do you want to eat?' I asked the boys.

'No,' said Harold.

'Why not?'

'Because the *bitok-bitok* is *busog*.'

We all dissolved in laughter. I was amused by his comical mixture of Ilonggo and English, but Harold was laughing at the meaning of what he had said — literally 'because the parasites are full.' Most of the food he ate, he said, was devoured by worms in his stomach.

The worms' diet didn't vary much. Rice was the staple of every meal, usually accompanied by vegetables and sometimes also by fish.

'Do you ever eat meat?'

'Only when have money,' said Harold.

'And then what kind of meat? Barbecued chicken?'

'Patty fig,' he said, with the Filipino's bewildering facility for treating the letters f and p as interchangeable.

We wandered slowly around the headland and back through the trees towards Marcelino's stall. It was time to head home.

'We evaporate,' said Amik, who really had been watching too many detective movies.

I had one last question for Harold.

'Are you happy living here?'

'Happy,' he said immediately, flashing a smile.

'Why? What do you like about this place?'

'Happy. Friends. Climbing the *lubi-lubi* — coconut trees. Swimming under the sea. Back dives.'

The simple pleasures of a childhood untarnished by the extravagances and complications of modern urban living. Life was hard, no question about it, but life was good.

In Negros, the *calachuchi* or frangipani tree is a symbol both of sadness and of happiness. It is commonly found in the island's graveyards where its spreading branches give mourners relief from the sun, but it is also used at fiesta time, when its fragrant flowers are woven into leis and worn by dancers.

There was a large *calachuchi* tree behind Marcelino's stall and it was covered in perfect white flowers.

A day which had started with sadness at the discovery of death had become a gentle celebration of life.

CHAPTER 2

Philippines, Negros Occidental
Hacienda Isabel

The Maglantay Family

Commitment to Change

When the price of sugar plunged in the late Eighties, the economic effects blew across Negros like a tornado, ripping families apart, snuffing out young lives and blowing away dreams. Poor families in the coastal towns and villages were buffeted by the side winds, but it was inland on the *haciendas* or sugar plantations that the full force of the storm was felt. The *sacadas* or sugar workers had no work, no income, no food.

The National Federation of Sugar Workers (NFSW), widely regarded as a trade union front for the communist New People's Army, devised one of the most practical solutions to the crisis, bringing the workers on each *hacienda* together and encouraging them to ask their *haciendero* or plantation owner for permission to use idle land to grow food for their families. Then, using money provided by overseas funding agencies, the NFSW got the workers started with tools, seeds, *carabaos* or water buffaloes and training. With fertile soil and a kind climate, the results could be dramatic. One *haciendero* gave his workers a rough and barren hillside and within five months they transformed it into a productive farm, growing corn, aubergines and squash. Food for hungry people, grown by hungry people.

In 1986 and 1987 I visited many of these communal farms and stayed with the sugar workers' families, listening to their stories, sleeping on the floors of their huts and learning about life in the raw. On one occasion a little girl died during the night and next morning her family simply dug a hole and buried her in a corner of a field because they couldn't afford a proper funeral. Death was part of everyday life.

One night I stayed on a plantation called Hacienda Isabel at the foot of Mount Kanla-on volcano in central Negros. It was a dangerous place, an area where government troops and the New People's Army often clashed. I stayed with one of the NFSW's extension workers, Enrique Maglantay, who lived and worked on the plantation with his wife Bellia and their four young children. My diary for that night read:

> *Night was closing in as we climbed the steps to Enrique's hut and gave his wife Bellia the food we had brought with us, to be included in the evening meal. Then by the light of two small candles we sat on the floor of the hut and talked.*
>
> *Enrique told us about the farm. Seventy-eight families were participating, and the corn harvest was not bad — each family received two sacks. The last crop of rice was forty-three sacks, the present crop was growing well and there was still some work on the plantation which brought in a little extra money. But it was difficult to make enough to feed and clothe four children. They were trying to persuade the owner to give them some more land.*
>
> *The military had been harassing the workers. A couple of*

weeks earlier they had come to the plantation and told the workers that they must go to the town hall to surrender. Their crime? Allegedly supporting the New People's Army.

'How can we give the NPA food when we don't even have enough for ourselves?' asked Enrique.

'So did you go to surrender?'

'They said they would ransack our homes if we didn't go, so we had no option. At the town hall they told us to stop making so many demands on the hacienda owner.'

I asked about Enrique and Bellia's hopes for their children. They said that all of them would study in primary school but they feared that none of them could go on to high school.

'As parents we want our children to finish studying, so that they will not be sugar workers any more. We want our children to have a better future, but poverty really means that we can do nothing,' said Enrique.

It would cost 500 pesos a year, or 25 dollars, to send one child to high school.

Working for Oxfam demands a commitment to change, and listening to Enrique talking about his family that evening I felt my own commitment renewed. A simple man, sitting on the floor of his home, propped against some sacks of corn with his two young sons clambering over him as we talked, he seemed to represent the universal father figure, wanting the best for his children. Heaven knows, his hopes are modest enough, but even they are dashed by the repression of poverty and a cruelly unjust system.

It began to rain heavily. We snuffed out the candles and fell asleep.

A few weeks later, Enrique sent me a photograph of his two young sons, Archie and Junryl. Six-year-old Archie looked pensive and slightly bewildered, but beside him four-year-old Junryl had his hands on his hips and a cheeky smile on his face, looking ready to take on the world. Enrique had scribbled a note saying, 'For Chris. To remind you of your visit to Hacienda Isabel.'

I carried that photo in my wallet for years. It did remind me. And eventually, after a gap of eleven years, it drew me back to Hacienda Isabel, in search of Enrique and Bellia and their boys.

The Same Old Story

Years of relative calm on the international sugar market had brought some respite after the hardships of the dark days, but even before leaving Bacolod to search for the Maglantays, I realized that fundamentally nothing had changed. The old injustices and hostilities were still there. Land reform hadn't happened and economic diversification hadn't worked. Negros still lived by sugar.

In a restaurant one evening I got talking to a young *haciendero*. He was in his early thirties, heir to a sugar kingdom, and had the arrogance of wealth. He wanted to tell me 'the real facts' about sugar.

'One condition,' he said, jabbing a finger towards my notebook. 'You don't name me.'

'Okay, but why not?'

'My father would kill me.'

For a moment, I thought he was about to spill the beans, to reveal some terrible scandal or to confess the exploitation of the hundreds of people employed by his family. But no. What followed was just the usual planters' tirade — blaming the government, cursing the communists, spitting at the workers. His father, I'm sure, would have echoed every word.

His workers, he said, were given free houses, free water, free electricity, free rice, free weddings, free baptisms, free burials and free land on which to grow their own food. What he didn't say was that they worked long hours in the cane fields for a wage so small that they couldn't even afford to send their children to secondary school.

'They can leave if they want to but they're lazy,' he said. 'Imagine if you're chief executive of a multinational company and they pay you one million dollars a year, with a house and a driver. Do you stay? Of course you do!'

I doubted whether Enrique would appreciate the comparison.

'People tell me the sugar industry in Negros has no future,' I said.

'They don't know what they're talking about. Sugar will always be here. It's a natural food. Can you imagine drinking Coke without sugar? Can you imagine eating a cake without sugar?'

No, he said, the problem was marketing.

'Can you imagine if the Chinese put just one spoonful of sugar into their tea? They would consume the Philippines' entire annual production of sugar in just two months.'

'Yes, but they'd ruin a good cup of Chinese tea.'

'No! Have you tried it? It's good.'

(I did and, believe me, it's not.)

For all his optimism, the young *haciendero* conceded that Negros could no longer rely on sugar alone and even said that his family would give up its sugar lands if the government offered a fair price.

'Look at where land reform has been successful,' he said. 'In Japan, the government paid cash. In Taiwan, the government paid cash. In Korea, if you didn't comply the government shot you. Here the government is offering twenty-five per cent of its valuation — *its* valuation, mind — in cash and the rest in bonds which can't be realized for ten years. What kind of a deal is that?'

And so he went on. The planters were being let down by their government and exploited by their workers. The same old moans being regurgitated eleven years on. Perhaps there was some truth in some of his complaints but I really couldn't be bothered to find out. The bottom line was that nothing had changed.

Back in the late Eighties, development agencies from all

over the world had queued up to help the sugar workers, and the Maglantays had had a procession of foreign aid workers sleeping on the floor of their hut. The communal farms programme, we had all thought, not only helped hungry people to feed themselves but would also lead to land reform and a radical redistribution of wealth. Such big dreams.

The programme had helped to stave off immediate famine and perhaps that was all the justification it needed, but it had clearly had little long-term impact. There had been a small measure of land reform but nothing fundamental, and all the talk of economic diversification had come to naught. Negros remained a monocrop economy and the mask of prosperity could not hide the underlying insecurity which still stalked the island.

Journey into Sugarland

The journey to find the Maglantays began shortly after eight o'clock one morning at Bacolod's southern bus terminus. Amik and I were looking for a ride to La Castellana in Central Negros, the town closest to Hacienda Isabel. He asked a few people who looked as though they ought to know, and then said what Filipinos always say when they haven't got a clue what is happening — 'For a while.'

So we waited for a while. A one-legged man propped himself against a bus and sold cigarettes from a wooden tray. A woman flashed a dazzling array of sunglasses in front of me and a newspaper vendor displayed the day's headlines. (*Negros Daily Bulletin:* 'Man takes rat poison, didn't die, hacks self'.) A jeep carrying policemen in combat gear swung into the forecourt and a young security guard paced sullenly around the throng of patient passengers, carrying a weapon which looked like a relic from the independence battles of the 1890s.

Amik suggested we board one of the waiting buses.

'Is it going to La Castellana?' I asked.

'Maybe.'

He steered me to a seat beside the rear door. 'We can jump,' he said, shaping his hands like a pistol and mimicking a hijacker.

The bus which should have been going to La Castellana

had apparently not arrived and nobody seemed to know why.

'If it doesn't arrive soon, this one will be obliged to go there. If it does arrive, we will transfer,' said Amik. 'We will wait for a while.'

So we waited. The day began to warm up and the smell of stale urine wafted in through the window. A boy led a blind man onto the bus and they passed from seat to seat, begging for money from passengers who stared out of the windows. A girl got off and went to buy herself an ice cream. Amik retreated to the air-conditioned convenience store. Almost an hour passed.

Then a second bus drew alongside, followed a minute later by a third. Amik reappeared and we transferred to one of the new arrivals.

'This one is going to La Castellana?' I ventured, more in hope than confidence.

'Maybe. If not, we transfer again.'

Just as I had resigned myself to an entire morning of bus-hopping around the terminal, a driver and a conductor appeared, both wearing freshly laundered white jackets and clearly ready for action. A man scrawled the bus's destination on the windscreen in white chalk, the engine spluttered into life and we were off.

The road ran south from Bacolod, down the western coast

of Negros, past fields planted with rice, but then we turned inland and the crops quickly changed, orchards of mango trees leading into mile after mile of fresh green sugar cane. Sugarland is not the flat, relentless landscape of the American prairies. It is softened by stands of coconut and banana trees and groves of bamboo, crisscrossed by streams meandering from the mountains to the sea, fringed with rice paddies. It is a lush, verdant place where you can almost hear the cane growing.

We left the bus at La Castellana and wandered into the cool dimness of the public market, hoping to buy some food to take to Bellia Maglantay. I suggested fish, so we wandered over to the fish stalls, but they were swarming with flies and the fish looked to have been a long time dead. I suggested vegetables. They too were covered with flies but we bought some anyway — beans, onions and garlic, as well as some vinegar, three tins of sardines and a large bag of mangoes.

'What about rice?' I asked.

Amik laughed. 'No need,' he said. 'They'll have plenty of rice.'

The market vendors explained that Hacienda Isabel was a good way out of town, on the road back to Bacolod, and so we took a jeepney and asked the driver to set us down at the entrance. Half an hour later we were standing on an empty road under a blazing sun, the jeepney disappearing into the distance and fields of sugar cane stretching away in every direction. We set off up a dirt track between two fields of tall canes, passing a few workers' huts and a barn full of clapped-out equipment — a rusty tractor, a jeep with no wheels.

A newer truck, loaded with sacks of fertilizer, came bumping down the track towards us, and a group of boys riding on top of the sacks waved excitedly and shouted, 'Hey, *tiyo* Romano!' I took a photograph as the truck rolled on down towards the road and then, as the dust scuffed up by its wheels settled, Amik called to me.

'Here is your friend.'

A small, slightly stooped man in shorts and a faded green vest walked towards me. Enrique Maglantay.

'Hello, Chris,' he said quietly. 'Welcome back.'

A Walk in the Shadows

Enrique was puzzled. Papa Joe, an old driver whom I had met by chance in Bacolod, had told him that I was back in Negros and was looking for him. But why had I come back after all these years? Was something wrong? What did I want? I, too, was confused. Enrique's home seemed to be in the wrong place, on the wrong side of the track and much smaller than I remembered.

So we sat on narrow benches at a wooden table, surrounded by curious children, and exchanged our stories of the past ten years.

Enrique explained that a few months after I visited in the summer of 1986, the military had stepped up their harassment. There were more raids on his home, more threats, more attacks.

'She was the one who saved me from the military,' he said, cuddling his ten-year-old daughter Iryn. 'When she was eight months old, they came searching my house again. They started punching and hitting me, but I held her close to me and so they had to stop.'

Enrique decided that his family was in danger and moved them to Sum-ag, on the outskirts of Bacolod. He found a job as an extension worker for a Catholic agency, helping sugar workers and small farmers and promoting the use of organic fertilizers. He had a regular income and was able to build his family a wooden hut on the bank of a river. Three more children were born and he and Bellia felt that things were going quite smoothly.

Then in 1994 the agency for which Enrique worked suddenly closed down. The family could not afford to stay in Sum-ag without a steady income and so decided to return home to Hacienda Isabel. Bellia moved first with four of the children, leaving the other three with Enrique in Sum-ag to continue their education. Enrique worked for a time as a construction worker in Bacolod, but a few weeks before our visit he had decided to move back to Isabel, bringing two more children with him. This time, he said, he had come home to stay.

'I like the family to all be together,' he said. 'I feel very happy when I see them.'

Coming home was not easy because Enrique and Bellia had given up their old hut on the *hacienda* and so had nowhere to live. Enrique built a new home, a small hut at the edge of a field, made of bamboo and thatched with nipa palm leaves.

The hut was home to nine people. It was raised from the ground and was basically one room, measuring about four metres by three. Half the room was a raised sleeping platform with the family's few possessions stacked in cardboard boxes at one end, together with a sack of rice. The other half was a living area by day and a second sleeping area by night. At one end was a shelf on which Bellia prepared and cooked food, and firewood was stacked neatly overhead. Another shelf ran down one side of the hut and

this was where the water jars were kept. There was no electricity, no running water, no toilet, no furniture. It was a completely functional home. No pictures on the walls, no ornaments, no trivial mementoes. Just an ancient guitar hanging in one corner.

'Who plays the guitar?' I asked Enrique. 'You?'

He raised his eyebrows in silent confirmation.

'But it has no strings,' he said quietly.

One of the benefits of coming home was that the four youngest daughters — Zorna, Iryn, Eralyn and Heyzie — could attend the elementary school on the next *hacienda*, barely a mile's walk away. The eldest daughter, nineteen-year-old Rona Marie, was, to her parents' great pride, away in Bacolod, studying commerce and management at a government college. But although her college was the cheapest they could find, the costs were still crippling and so her two brothers, Archie and Junryl, the boys whose photo I had kept all these years, had been pulled out of school.

Archie, now a couple of weeks away from his seventeenth birthday, had become a young man. He had his father's quiet and serious manner; the two of them behaved together more

like brothers than father and son. It was three years since Archie had been to school, although he still harboured hopes of returning one day and studying to become a motor mechanic. Until then, he worked in the fields, alongside his parents.

Fourteen-year-old Junryl was quite tall for his age and his skin was darker than Archie's. He hoped to study at college and become an electrician but knew there would be no school for him for at least a year.

Enrique confirmed that the impressions created by that old photograph were correct.

'Archie is very quiet, Junryl is very talkative,' he said. 'Archie is the hardworking one. He helps us and when he earns money he gives some to his sister so that she can finish her college. Junryl knows how to earn money but sometimes he... um... forgets to share it.'

Junryl had spent ten of his fourteen years at Sum-ag and so was more accustomed to the semi-urban environment than to the tranquillity of the *hacienda*. He was not happy about returning to the countryside. His friends were all in Sum-ag and he said the food there was 'more balanced.'

Enrique smiled and said, 'He can earn some money there, that's why he prefers it. He can walk around selling iced *buko* salad and sometimes make 30 *pesos* in a day, or he can go down to the seashore in the morning and collect some shellfish to sell in Sum-ag market for 15 *pesos*.'*

As we sat outside the hut exchanging our stories, a crowd of curious cousins and children pressed round us, wanting to hear what Enrique and '*tiyo* Romano' were talking about, but eventually Enrique suggested that the two of us go for a walk around the *hacienda* on our own.

Ten years ago I had arrived there at dusk, slept through a night of torrential rain and left soon after first light, but this time in the bright sunshine of a golden afternoon I saw the stunning beauty of a timeless landscape with clean air and clear light.

We stopped beside some fields of bright green rice. During the crisis ten years ago, the workers had been given this patch of ground and together they had built an intricate maze of irrigation channels to guide water from the moun-

* US$1 = 40 *pesos*

43

tain streams through the paddies.

'But then we had some trouble,' said Enrique. 'The military said that if we were working together and sharing the rice we must be communists. So now each family has a few small fields — but we still help each other, so really nothing has changed.'

The Maglantays harvested three crops a year from their fields but Enrique said it wasn't enough to feed a young and hungry family. I felt embarrassed that we hadn't brought some rice with us and remembered Amik's confident assurance in the market that there would be plenty here. Even he had not realized quite how close to the edge the *sacadas* lived.

We walked down to the Buhangim River, which was little more than a stream after the long dry summer months. A few men and boys were digging sand from the river bed and loading it onto a waiting lorry. It was tough work, paying just 70 *pesos* per square metre of sand, but Enrique said it paid better than field work.

Field work meant planting the cane, weeding the fields through the growing season, applying fertilizers and cutting back the grass along the tracks that wove through the *hacienda*. Then at harvest  time the *sacadas* wrapped themselves up in old clothes until only their faces were visible and began the backbreaking work of cutting the cane by hand and loading it onto trucks which took it away for milling. They started work at six o'clock in the morning and worked until ten, when they stopped for lunch. The afternoon shift was from twelve until four, and for eight hours' work they were paid 84 *pesos*, well below the official minimum wage. For most of the year there was enough work to employ each worker for only two or three days a week, and in the so-called 'dead season' during the summer there was virtually no work at all. That was when meat disappeared from the diet and families lived

on vegetables and root crops, sometimes just rice with salt.

Yet the workers' principal demand was not for more pay or better working conditions but for more land on which to grow rice, corn and vegetables to feed themselves and their families. They had been given some land but it wasn't enough.

'How much land does a family need to be able to feed itself?' I asked.

Enrique thought for a time. 'It depends on the size of the family,' he said, 'but you could say three hectares.'

'But,' I pointed out, 'if every family was given three hectares there would be no land left for sugar.'

'If the whole of Negros is filled with rice and corn, I think that is the key to development.'

'So although you are a sugar worker, you want to see the sugar industry die.'

'Compare the sugar and the rice. It's better that rice is wider than sugar because rice is the number one need of the people here. So why don't we plant rice wider than sugar?'

More than fifty families lived at Hacienda Isabel but their huts were scattered all over the place, with no more than five or six clustered together in any one place. We walked on into the next valley, where a man with a *carabao* was ploughing a tiny plot beside the river. Around another corner, a man was admiring his collection of fighting cocks, birds on which many days' wages would be gambled; 'the sickness of the Philippines,' muttered Enrique. Up the next rise, a young mother and her baby stood watching as father prepared a plot of land in front of their hut for growing vegetables.

'Many foreigners came to the *hacienda* back in 1986,' said Enrique, 'but no foreigner has ever been this far.'

We walked for a while in silence as the afternoon shadows lengthened into evening.

Then Enrique added, 'So many foreign aid workers came to visit us in those days and stayed in my home, and it was difficult for me because the other people on the *hacienda* thought I was getting something for myself. You know that I wasn't. We just wanted people to understand the sugar workers' situation.'

'I'm sorry,' I said. 'Is this difficult for you now, having me here?'

He smiled. 'Don't worry about it.'

By the time we arrived home, it was dark and Amik and Archie had set off to search for us, so we sat down to wait for them. Iryn and Heyzie climbed onto Enrique's lap and he proudly showed me Iryn's school report card.
She had achieved an average of 87.51, missed only four days schooling in the year and had never been late.

'My first daughter got a rating of 87.4 for her first year in college,' Enrique said proudly.

'Archie and Junryl both got a general rating of 78 before they had to stop,' added Bellia.

Amik and Archie finally emerged from the darkness and

we sat on the floor of the hut for a meal of rice, sardines and beans, followed by sweet mangoes.

Enrique mentioned that he had recently stood in the *barangay* elections, one of forty-seven candidates in a huge constituency that covered twenty-eight *haciendas*. Campaigning was a nightmare with such vast distances to be covered and he had been able to spend only three days canvassing support because he couldn't afford to miss work. Even so, he had finished third, just two hundred votes behind the winner.

'I lost because of money,' he said. No bitterness, just a statement of fact.

When families were short of cash, Enrique explained, they could get an advance from a money lender and then repay their debt after the next rice harvest, but interest rates were extortionate — to borrow 100 *pesos* for three months cost one sack of rice, which was worth 350 *pesos*.

'Sometimes after your harvest you just rub your hands together like this because you have nothing left. It has all gone to pay back your debts.'

'Will you have to use any of your next harvest to repay debts?'

'Two sacks. But maybe I will need to borrow some more to pay for school enrolments.'

The wind began to blow, bending the tall canes around the hut, and a grey curtain of rain swept across the fields towards us. A passing neighbour named Rodolfo came in to take shelter, accompanied by two of his daughters and a bottle of whisky. Rodolfo had had a few too many but happily helped himself to a few more, as his daughters sat dutifully and silently beside him. While he bantered with Enrique and Amik and the rain pounded the palm leaves, I sat in a corner and talked to Bellia.

She and Enrique had known each other since childhood. They had both been born on the *hacienda* and six of her brothers and sisters still lived there. She was a calm and capable woman, concerned solely with the well-being of her family.

'The situation now is very terrible compared to the last ten years because most of the things are very expensive,' she said. 'Last ten years my children were only four — now it's seven. And Enrique do not have permanent work. If I can afford to finish my daughter and my sons can go to school, I am very happy.'

Bellia worked alongside her husband and son in the cane fields, helped in the family's rice paddies, cared for the home and looked after seven children. Yet despite the hardship of her life there, she drew a mother's comfort from being back on the *hacienda* after seven years in the urban environment of Sum-ag.

'In Sum-ag, if you have no money you cannot eat, but here you can pick some vegetables,' she said.

The rain stopped and Rodolfo and his patient daughters rose to leave. Amik, now with his shirt stripped off, a bandana tied round his head and cigarette burning low in his fingers, lifted the lamp to light their way. '*Hasta la vista*, babies,' he called, as they disappeared into the night.

Enrique explained that Rodolfo's wife had died three years earlier, leaving him with nine children.

'Nine!' I repeated with evident surprise.

'His father had seventeen. *Only* seventeen! There is a family on the upper part of the *hacienda* with *only* twenty-four. When there was a competition for the family with the most children, of course they won because they had two dozen! They all went to elementary school but none of them went to high school.'

'The mother is my godmother,' added Bellia. 'She is a very small woman.'

'*Pinoy talaga*,' said Enrique, 'that is the Filipino for you.'

Kapalaran

Late in the evening, when the children and Amik had fallen asleep and Bellia was finishing her chores, Enrique and I sat on the floor of the hut with just a flickering oil lamp between us. The setting was almost identical to the scene of our conversation eleven years earlier, but as he spoke softly into the night I realized that Enrique had changed. The years had not been kind to my old friend and he spoke so softly that at times I could hardly hear him. He was older, quieter and wiser than before, still careful and sober in what he said,  thinking about each answer and taking care not to exaggerate or misrepresent, but just occasionally showing a trace of the disappointment of a man who knew that his die had been cast.

After many years as an agricultural extension worker, initially for a trade union and then for a non-governmental agency, Enrique questioned how much these overseas-funded programmes had achieved.

'When you just educate people about farming without any implementation there is no development,' he said. 'Or, if there is, it is development of the agency's own staff. You don't really need to teach Filipino people about agriculture because they already know. What they need is not education — it's capital for materials.'

I pointed out that many grants had included money for capital costs.

'I know, I've seen the proposals to the funding agencies. 'Ten *carabaos* will be distributed to the landless workers, fifty heads of pig, one hundred ducks' — but there are no *carabaos*, there are no pigs, no ducks.'

'Are you saying that agencies are corrupt?'

'If there is corruption in the government there is also corruption among the non-government agencies.'

I asked what was the most urgent need in Negros, the top priority for funding — agriculture, the environment, health, mother and child care, education, livelihood programmes, the elderly... the list of possibilities was endless.

Enrique thought for a while before answering.

'Education,' he said finally. 'Helping children to finish their education.'

'Why?'

'Because education is the only way that people can get away from this life.'

Enrique himself had been one of five children and his father had died when he was young. He had completed high school in La Castellana but the family had been unable to afford college fees.

'So I could not achieve my ambition,' he said. 'More than eighty per cent of children can finish elementary school, but probably only five per cent can afford high school and at college I think it is only one per cent.'

This was why Enrique had always been so keen for his

children to complete a full education — it was an achievement which most sugar workers' children could not hope to match and one which he himself had been denied. Ten years earlier he had feared that none of his children would be able to attend high school, yet Rona Marie had not only completed high school but had even gone on to college. No wonder he and Bellia were so very proud of her.

But what about the boys, Archie and Junryl, whose education had been curtailed?

It wasn't unusual, Enrique said, for children to drop out of education for a few years. He had done it himself. The boys' cousin, Wilfred, who was twenty, was about to go back to school after missing three years. The plan was for Rona Marie to complete her education first and then to get a good job so that she could support her brothers, who in turn would graduate and support their four younger sisters. Of course, it wasn't the ideal arrangement and it hurt his heart to watch Archie working in the cane fields at such a young age, but his ambition for his sons — indeed, for all his children — was the same as it had been eleven years earlier. The dream had been delayed but he and Bellia would continue their struggle to make it come true.

'I have not lost my hope,' he said.

When I asked how much money it would take to get Archie and Junryl back to school, Enrique said that enrolment fees and school uniforms were not the main problem. What poor families could not afford were the daily expenses of jeepney rides and eating away from home. Archie and Junryl would have go to school in La Castellana, which was seven and a half kilometres away, and the jeepney fare would be four *pesos* each way. Each of them would need 12 *pesos* a day to buy food. That worked out at 4,400 *pesos* per boy per year.

'But the parents can contribute something,' said Enrique.

'Well, suppose Archie and Junryl were given scholarships of 2,000 *pesos* each per year. Would you send them back to school?'

'Yes. Why not?'

So there was the bottom line. Two boys whose education was being at best delayed and possibly stopped altogether for the sake of 2,000 *pesos* per year. About 50 dollars. It seemed so little and yet to Enrique and Bellia it would make all the difference.

The lamp was almost out of oil. It was time to sleep. Enrique went outside to urinate while I sat on the floor, thinking about the boys' situation. When he came back into the hut, he looked at me and smiled.

'Chris, don't worry too much about our problems. This is our *kapalaran* — I don't know how to say in English.'

Destiny.

Hong Kong

Ho Yun Chiu

Man Hurt in Crash

Before joining Oxfam, I used to produce documentary films for a Hong Kong television station and in 1981 we decided to mark 'The Year of the Disabled' with a series of programmes showing how people coped with disability. One film was to show how an accident victim could be helped to reconstruct his or her life and I went to explain the idea to Maureen Wagg, senior physiotherapist at the Margaret Trench Rehabilitation Centre. We wanted to film the entire course of one person's rehabilitation, from Day One right through to discharge, but Mrs. Wagg hesitated. The emotional trauma of sudden disability and the sheer physical effort of rehabilitation meant that her patients were under enough stress without us invading their lives with microphones, cameras and bright lights.

A few weeks later, however, she called to say that she had found a young man who had been admitted to the centre three

months earlier and who seemed to have a very calm tempera-
ment and positive outlook. He had had some medical problems
but his rehabilitation was about to start and she had discussed
with him the idea of allowing us to film his progress. The man
had agreed.

Four months later the film of his rehabilitation was
screened on Hong Kong television. It was called *Man Hurt in
Crash* and this was how it began:

November 14, 1980

*There was a serious traffic accident on Cas-
tle Peak Road in the early hours of this morning.
A goods vehicle crashed into a stationary lorry
near the 21 Milestone. The collision was very
violent and both vehicles were badly damaged.*

*Eight people were injured and one of them,
a twenty-one year old man, is now in Princess
Margaret Hospital with serious leg injuries.*

Then the film jumped forward six months.

June 1, 1981

This is the man with serious leg injuries — Ho Yun Chiu.

*He was a passenger in the goods vehicle and at the time of
the crash was asleep with his legs stretched out under the front
seats. He was rushed to hospital and one leg was immediately
amputated. A couple of days later a doctor explained to him that
his life would be in danger unless the other leg was also amputated, so it too was cut off.*

*Chiu is number five in a family of eight, living at home in
Un Chau Estate in Sham Shui Po. Before the accident he had
tried a number of jobs and at the time of the crash was working*

as a delivery man. He was a keen sportsman, particularly enjoy-
ing football and swimming.

Today, six months after the accident, that past life lies in
pieces. He cannot go back to his old job, he cannot walk, even his
family home has become inaccessible to him.

Thinking back, Chiu remembers what a terrible shock it
was to realize that he had lost both his legs. He was in a very bad
mood, but he's proud to say that he never cried in front of his
family — even though, he says, he was weeping in his heart.

We filmed Chiu countless times as he set about building a
new life for himself. We watched him learning to bandage his
stumps, lifting weights to improve his upper body strength,
learning industrial sewing, being fitted for his new legs and
taking his first tentative steps. He tackled every exercise with
tremendous enthusiasm. In one sequence in the swimming
pool, a rubber ring was placed around his waist and then tied to
the side of the pool, so that no matter how hard he swam he remained in the same place. The physiotherapist said it was the
most soul-destroying of exercises and that he had never seen
anyone attack it with so much determination.

Apart from being held up for a few days by a troublesome
sinus in one stump, Chiu's physical rehabilitation went extraordinarily smoothly, but his emotional healing was harder to
judge because he was a man of few words. Conversations were
confined to pleasantries and, while some patients wore their
hearts on their sleeves, Chiu kept his locked well away from
public gaze. He dealt with the trauma of losing his legs quietly
and privately. A man of gruff determination.

We went with an occupational therapist to see a flat which
the Housing Authority had offered to Chiu's family. It needed

to be accessible to him when he was wearing his artificial legs and when he used a wheelchair, but there were steps into the building, steps into the flat, even steps into the toilet. The place was hopeless and indicated the problems Chiu could expect as a disabled person in crowded, hilly Hong Kong.

The film ended on the day that he was discharged from the centre. We showed him walking confidently and even managing to get himself onto a minibus, but the positive pictures were tempered by a warning from Mrs Wagg.

The main physical battle of learning to cope with new legs is behind him and he's done very, very well, but he's got a tremendous step to take on leaving the rehab centre and going out into the world for the first time and being accepted back into the community. This takes quite a lot of strength on the part of the patient and needs a lot of moral support from his family. He has really got to be a strong character to push and make a place for himself again now as a disabled person once he leaves us.

That was 1981.

Sixteen years later in 1997 I decided to go looking for Chiu, to see how he had coped.

Acceptance

I had no idea where Chiu was or what had happened to him.

The only clue was that a few years earlier I had spotted him across a crowded restaurant during a banquet organized by the Hong Kong Sports Association for the Physically Disabled.

It was a pretty tenuous lead, but I started my search by going to the Association's office and asking whether Chiu was a member. He was, and a few hours later, with his agreement, the Association gave me his telephone number.

It was as easy as that. Typical Hong Kong. Quick and efficient.

I called the number, expecting to have to muddle through in Cantonese, but the woman who answered spoke perfect English. She introduced herself as Chiu's wife, Francesca, and said that her husband was sleeping after working overnight. I explained who I was and a few days later we all met up in a coffee shop, a few miles from where Chiu and his family lived in a flat on the twenty-fifth floor of a government housing estate.

Francesca arrived first with their daughters, twelve-year-old Veronica and seven-year-old Paula. Then Chiu walked in.

'He's put on too much weight, hasn't he?' said Francesca as he came towards us.

Certainly he was heavier than I remembered, but otherwise he seemed remarkably unchanged after sixteen years.

'Nay ho?' he said. How are you? 'Ho loy mo geen.' Long time, no see.

The girls went off to play and we settled down to talk. It was July 1, 1997 and the previous evening people around the world had watched as Hong Kong was handed back to China. In pouring rain, the Union Jack had been lowered for the last time and then, on the stroke of midnight, the flags of China and the Hong Kong Special Administrative Region had fluttered into life, symbolizing the reunification of Hong Kong and her motherland.

I mentioned the ceremonies to Chiu but he had seen nothing of them. He had been working all night, driving a taxi around the streets of Kowloon. A very lucrative shift it had been, too. There were so many people out and about that he had taken twice as much as on a normal night.

'Did you listen to the ceremonies on the radio?' I asked.

'Yes,' he said.

'What did you feel?'

'Nothing special. We just have to accept it.'

Unemotional and pragmatic. Again, typical Hong Kong. Typical Chiu.

Francesca added, 'He has no political interest. He doesn't really think about the future.' She laughed. 'I think most men are like that.'

During our many visits to film at the rehabilitation centre sixteen years earlier we had completely missed the fact that

Chiu was becoming fond of one of the other patients, an eighteen-year-old girl who was also recovering from an accident which had left her confined to a wheelchair — Francesca.

'He left the rehab centre two weeks before I did,' she said, 'and when he left I didn't know how I would manage. You know, he'd been my buddy — although I wasn't really his buddy at that stage!'

Their relationship flourished and the buddies became husband and wife, but on meeting them together this first time I was reminded of a principle from schoolboy physics — like poles repel, unlike poles attract. Francesca was bubbly and talkative, always laughing and joking. I would ask Chiu a question and she would answer for him, not in a domineering way but simply because she knew his thoughts and could express them more clearly. She was Portuguese, completely fluent in both English and Cantonese, and worked for an international hotel chain. Chiu, by contrast, was more reserved and serious, almost dour. His Cantonese answers to my many questions were short and straightforward, no messing about.

But appearances were deceptive.

'He's the optimist,' said Francesca, later. 'You know me, I like to joke a lot, but it's a kind of therapy for me because I feel very unhappy inside. I think that in life you have to fight every day.

'Everybody said we wouldn't work out, with both of us being handicapped, but even though the times were difficult we tried to work it out. I used to cry a lot but he was the hard stone, the bannister. I used to worry about what would happen but he would say, "Don't worry. If no one will help us, we'll always have ourselves." We were very determined that we had to get married and that we had to have children. We always  console ourselves that the bad part of life is that we had our accidents, but the good part is that we met each other.'

Casting his mind back, Chiu reckoned Mrs. Wagg had been right to warn how difficult it would be to leave the rehabilitation centre and go out into the world as a disabled person for the first time.

'I was very scared,' he said. 'I didn't know what to do. I had no job, I had no money, I'd had no education. I didn't know how my family were going to help me. My parents, especially my mother, were very sad. She kept crying and I had to console her.'

The family was eventually given a ground floor flat which was accessible to Chiu, both in his wheelchair and on crutches, but every time he went out he was very conscious of people looking at him.

'Even now people still stare,' he said, 'but ten years ago it was much worse because there were not many handicapped people coming out.'

Chiu's former employer paid him a token salary for a time and he also received some insurance money, so the year after leaving the centre he was able to open a noodle shop in partnership with three able-bodied friends. Chiu worked as the cashier and for the first few years the business went well. Chiu learned to drive and in 1984 he and Francesca were married. Their first daughter, Veronica, was born.

But then the business started to decline. Two of his partners left and Chiu had to become the cook as well as the cashier. He and his last remaining partner struggled on for a time but eventually, staring bankruptcy in the face, they had to close down. It was a bitter blow, the only moment since his accident when Chiu really felt that he had hit rock bottom. His employment, his hopes and his security all disappeared.

'Losing the business must have seemed like a second accident,' I said to Chiu.

'That's right,' he said. 'It was the worst time in all these years.'

'Life has really forced him to go on,' said Francesca. 'After the accident he thought he had lost everything, and then he built up the business and had something, and then — down again. But he has a wife who is disabled and two children. He has to keep going.'

Chiu decided to make a new start and to work for a taxi driver's licence. He achieved his goal in 1993 and had been driving ever since. There were thirteen taxis in Hong Kong which were specially adapted to be driven by people who did not have the use of their legs, and all were individually owned and operated by disabled people. Most were running twenty-four hours a day, with different drivers taking different shifts.

Chiu was a relief driver, helping out when others were not available, working the overnight shift from six o'clock at night until six o'clock the next morning. Driving at night was much easier, he said, with no traffic jams and fewer restrictions on where he could pick up and drop off passengers.  After four years, he still enjoyed his work, and most passengers, sitting in the back seat and paying little attention to the driver's controls, had no idea that he was disabled.

The trouble was that he couldn't earn enough money. He worked only when other regular drivers wanted a night off, and on average drove only three or four nights a week. More than half of the money he took in fares went to pay for his hire of the taxi and for petrol. He dreamed of having his own taxi and being his own boss, saying he would feel much more secure, but the finances were daunting — a licence would cost about HK$3.4 million*, which meant that he would need a deposit of HK$600,000 and would then have to stump up HK$30,000 per month in repayments. That was an awful lot of fares.

As I jotted down the figures in my notebook, I couldn't help wondering what the Flores family back in Punta Taytay or Enrique Maglantay at Hacienda Isabel would make of them. If Enrique worked in the cane fields for a hundred years he still wouldn't have enough for even the deposit. Not that Chiu was a rich man. Hong Kong was simply a very expensive city.

'So what do you think the chances are that you'll be able to get your own taxi one day?'

Chiu thought for a long time.

'Fifty-fifty,' he said.

* US$1 = HK$7.8

Playing Hard

As a teenager, Chiu had been keen on football and swimming, but while in the rehabilitation centre recovering from his accident he was introduced to wheelchair basketball and took to it like a duck to water. At first, he played because he wanted something to occupy his mind and to speed his recovery, but he went on to develop a genuine enthusiasm for the sport and, sixteen years on, still returned to the centre twice a week to train with a group of friends.

'It's the only sport I like,' said Chiu. 'When I'm playing I can forget everything and just concentrate on the game. I like being in a team of people, all working together — but I also enjoy the moment when I can shoot the ball into the basket.'

Knowing nothing about wheelchair basketball, I went to the centre and met senior physiotherapist Chan Sai Hong, the man who had introduced Chiu to the sport and who still

coached him and his friends. He explained that the rules were much the same as for basketball played by able-bodied people, with each team having five players on court at one time, but that disabled players were graded from one to five according to the severity of their disabilities. Chiu was graded three.

Mr. Chan wanted players with power, balance, endurance and speed. Upper body strength was vital and training sessions involved weight training and endless sprints, powering wheelchairs up and down the court, building up the chest and triceps. Most of the players were men in their twenties or thirties, who had been disabled by polio or had lost limbs in accidents or as a result of cancer. One man had fainted at a railway station, fallen onto the track and a train had run over his leg.

'Most of them have a pretty positive attitude towards life,' said Mr. Chan.

'How do you rate Chiu?' I asked.

'He can shoot and he's got big hands so he can catch the ball. His balance is not so good, but then you'd expect that because he's a three-point player.' He paused. 'But he's slow.'

'Really?' I said, surprised. 'He's built like a bull. His upper body looks very powerful.'

'That's not power, that's fat,' said Mr. Chan. 'I've told him about it for years, but it's difficult for him because in his job he's sitting down all day.'

Despite his weight problem, Chiu had taken his sport seriously and had gradually worked his way into contention for a place in the national team, until in 1989, nine years after his accident, he was actually selected to play for Hong Kong. He had gone on to establish himself as a regular member of the team and, as well as playing in international matches at home, had represented Hong Kong in competitions in China, Japan and Macau.

'How did it feel the first time you went out to play for Hong Kong?' I asked.

Chiu drew his hand across his chin and looked slightly embarrassed.

'I was very happy,' he said, 'very proud to be a Hong Kong player. I still am very proud. There are not many chances to represent Hong Kong and the life of a sportsman is really short.'

In 1994 Chiu had an accident in Beijing, falling out of his wheelchair and knocking himself unconscious. Just as he was getting over that injury, he dislocated his shoulder at work. It was almost two years before he resumed playing and he lost his place in the Hong Kong side.

Yet despite his comment that a sportsman's life was short, Chiu at thirty-seven was still training hard. He was eight

months into his comeback and unwilling to accept that his international career was over. He reckoned he still had a chance to play for Hong Kong and was about to join his friends on a training trip to Japan, to learn new techniques from a renowned Japanese coach.

Before that, there were more strenuous sessions with coach Chan, who was known for standing no nonsense and for pushing his players to the limit. Some liked his coaching methods, others did not.

'You've seen the training,' said Francesca. 'It's hell. It's like you're a G.I. He doesn't allow smoking or drinking, no swearing on the court, no talking back, but there's a group of them who are willing to take it.'

They trained twice a week, using the rehab centre's small outdoor court and its gymnasium, but once a month the players clubbed together and rented an indoor games hall, to give themselves more practice on a full-sized court. The hall was on a hillside, overlooking the factories and densely packed apartment blocks of east Kowloon, and I went to watch a training session. Most of the players had already done an hour and a half's pre-training at the rehab centre, but Chiu and Francesca had been away on a weekend camp with their daughters. They were the last to arrive and Chiu

quickly took off his legs, still clad in jeans, and settled himself into his sporting wheelchair.

It was a rough, tough workout. The training exercises were very strenuous and the game which followed was fast and furious. The marking of players was very tight, with plenty of collisions and locking of wheels. Wheelchairs overturned and players were thrown out onto the court.

There was one young man who had lost a leg to cancer. His hair was tied back in a short ponytail and he stripped off his shirt to reveal a well-developed chest and arms. In training sprints, when everyone had to race the length of the court, he invariably won. He was a real athlete, very focused, and Mr. Chan described him as 'an uncut gem'. In the last minutes of the practice game, he collided with another player and was thrown out of his wheelchair in front of me and for a few seconds struggled desperately to get back into his chair. It was a horrible moment, an illusion shattered. Watching him training and playing, I had completely forgotten about his disability and had seen him simply as an athlete, but now it seemed that the reality was this helpless person lying on the court at my feet, flapping about like a fish out of water.

Then I thought again. Why was I defining him by his disability? Why was his inability to pick himself up more important than his many abilities? When he was in his wheelchair, straining every muscle to win a sprint or stretching to prevent an opponent from shooting for the basket, that was who he really was, a fit, handsome and highly motivated man.

The other players quickly came to his aid, helped him back into his chair and the game continued, shouts echoing around the hall.

Chiu broke clear of his marker and raced down the righthand side of the court, calling for the ball and watching it loop across the court towards him. His calloused hands stopped the wheelchair within a couple of yards. He caught the ball, sat up straight and steadied himself for a split second before shooting for the basket. The ball teetered on the ring and fell in.

Chiu turned, sweat pouring down his face, and wheeled off down the court, a picture of concentration, training hard, still trying to regain his place in the Hong Kong team.

Facing It

We arranged to have lunch together. I told Francesca that I wanted to ask Chiu not just about facts but about feelings.

'You won't get much out of him,' she said.

I laughed.

'No, really. He's very shy.'

We sat around a table in a Chinese restaurant and watched the rain teeming down outside. It had been raining every day for the past month. We wondered if it would ever stop.

'Bad for business,' said Chiu.

I told him that my overriding memory from sixteen years earlier was of the quietly determined way in which he had tackled every task the physiotherapists had set for him. Nothing had seemed to throw him off balance. Mrs. Wagg had described him as a model patient.

'Was that just my impression or were you really so determined?' I asked.

'I was like that even before the accident,' he said, 'and when I knew there was a chance to walk again, that made me even more determined.'

'Mrs. Wagg said you seemed to be a very strong character.'

'I don't know if I'm a strong character, but I had to face it. I had lost my legs. But then I had the hope that I could learn to walk again. Maybe that hope made me more strong. The survival instinct was very high. The only thing I wanted to do was to survive. My legs were gone. They were gone, there was nothing I could do about it.'

I wondered whether people who had been friends with him before his accident had drifted away after he was disabled, but he said that he still had a few of his old able-bodied friends and that some of them had been very helpful to him when he was first discharged from the rehab centre. He reckoned that, of his friends now, half were disabled and half were able-bodied. Francesca disagreed, saying most were disabled, but Chiu seemed reluctant to concede the point.

Eventually he said, 'I wouldn't say that all my friends are disabled, but most are.'

'Do you feel more relaxed when you're with disabled friends?'

'Yes. I feel happier if the whole group is disabled, rather than having to go into a restaurant full of able-bodied people and have everyone staring at me.'

I filled Chiu's tea cup and he tapped the table in acknowledgment.

It was hard, he said, to generalize about people's attitudes. Some people were rude and some patronizing, but most were fine. Older people were the most insensitive.

'When I am trying to get into the car or walking along the street, I hate people just staring at me, being nosey, gossiping.'

Francesca added with a smile, 'Sometimes when he helps

me get into the car people will just stand there and watch, so when I get in I open the window and say "Please clap now, the show's over." That always gets them!'

The waitress removed the lid of the teapot and poured an arc of scalding hot water onto the tea leaves.

I said, 'The shock and disappointment of being suddenly disabled are too much for some people to bear and they become very bitter or even take their own lives.'

Chiu nodded.

'Did you ever consider suicide?'

'Never,' he said firmly.

'Did you have a religious faith to help you come to terms with what had happened?'

'No.'

'Do you feel any bitterness towards the man who was driving?'

'No, I've never had that feeling. It was an accident.'

'So it really is behind you now? No bad dreams?'

'I mainly think about the present and the future,' said Chiu. 'It's really a long time ago.'

His youngest daughter Paula was getting bored listening to Daddy answering questions. The waitress was waiting to move in and clear the plates. It was time to head back out into the rains.

I looked at Chiu across the table.

'You remember in the film how Mrs. Wagg said you would have to be a really strong character to build a new place for yourself in the community as a disabled person?'

He nodded.

'Well, look at you now. You're married, you have two lovely daughters, you have a home, you have a job — okay, not as good a job as you want but still it's a job — you have good friends and you've represented Hong Kong in international sport. You've done it, haven't you?'

He looked down at the table cloth, turned his tea cup around, slightly embarrassed. Then he looked up at me and smiled.

'Yes,' he said. 'I have.'

National Pride

Three months later Hong Kong hosted an international wheelchair basketball competition with teams from Guangzhou, Taipei, Macau and Hong Kong. For the first time in two years, Chiu was selected for the Hong Kong squad, but as the competition started it remained to be seen whether he would actually be chosen to play.

I was back in Hong Kong for a few days and went along, expecting all the razzle-dazzle of a big sporting occasion — crowds of spectators, cheerleaders, television lights and photographers. Instead, the teams did battle in a cavernous hall, watched by a few officials and a couple of dozen wives and girlfriends. Almost no spectators, almost no media coverage. It felt more like a midweek practice session than an international tournament.

Not that the players seemed to mind. The matches were fiercely contested.

Hong Kong's first clash was against Macau. Chiu sat on the sidelines, yelling encouragement, as five other players took Hong Kong into an early lead. Then the coach decided to make a substitution. One player came off court and Chiu was told to go on. A proud smile crossed his face as he removed his shirt to reveal a vest saying 'Hong Kong'.

He had waited for this moment for almost three years, ever since his accident in Beijing, and he wasn't going to waste it. He threw himself into the play. His eyes darted around the court, trying to spot chances. He yelled at his teammates to give him the ball and sweat poured down his face. He scored six points as Hong Kong thrashed Macau by sixty-four points to six.

Chiu wasn't selected for the tournament's later matches and could only sit and suffer as his teammates went down to Guangzhou by thirty points to thirty-one in a heart-stopping final. Still, it was a start. Two years after his injury, one year after resuming training and at the advanced age of thirty-seven, he was back in international competition.

Another setback overcome, another battle won.

CHAPTER 4

Thailand, Klong Toey

Wittaya Buitsak

An Uneasy Relationship

I became involved with Wittaya Buitsak almost by accident and certainly against my better judgement.

It all started in Klong Toey, Bangkok's biggest slum, home to more than seventy thousand people and a place with a terrible reputation. Few Bangkok residents and even fewer tourists step inside Klong Toey's crowded alleys, but in 1989 I went there to visit the Duang Prateep Foundation, which organized educational sponsorships for slum children.

I was a sceptical guest. Child sponsorship schemes are popular with donors but many development agencies avoid them, arguing that helping communities is more effective than helping individuals, that singling out a few children for sponsorship can be unfair and divisive, that sponsorship schemes are difficult and expensive to administer and that they foster outdated concepts of dependency. I had a head full of such prejudices.

The Foundation's staff introduced their work, which even then was helping more than two thousand children and their families, and it was hard not to be impressed. At a Duang Prateep kindergarten, dozens of four- and five-year-olds, dressed in simple uniforms, stood up as we entered their classrooms and shouted *'Sawasdee'* — Welcome. The Foundation's staff said there was no shortage of sponsors wanting to help these little ones but that finding support for tertiary students, who didn't look so sweet and whose tuition fees were much higher, was more difficult, sometimes even impossible. Perhaps that was hardly surprising, but I was appalled. Klong Toey children who had qualified to study at university level were, almost by definition, pretty special and deserved support. So, forgetting all my well-rehearsed objections, I offered to sponsor one.

Back in Hong Kong a few weeks later, a letter arrived introducing 'Vittaya Pudsak' as a young person needing help. That

spelling of his name, incidentally, was the first of many versions to appear over the next few years — in addition to Vittaya Pudsak, we had Vitaya, Wittaya and Witthaya, Budsak, Bootsak, Buitsak and Buithsak. The changes had no significance, of course — his name was, is and always will be วิทยา บุตรศักดิ์.

Wittaya was twenty years old. He had been helped by the Foundation during his secondary school years but had then stopped studying because his family couldn't afford to send him to university. He wanted to study mass communications but needed a scholarship of 6,000 *baht* (then about 230 dollars) per year to pay for his tuition. His father was unwell and the family depended on his mother, who earned a couple of thousand *baht* per month by selling *khanum toey*, tiny coconut desserts which she made in bowls not much bigger than thimbles and sold from a barrow in the slum.

These personal details about Wittaya and his family were interesting, but in a sense they were also irrelevant. If the Foundation had introduced a girl studying hotel management or a boy training to be a seaman my response would have been the same. The aim was simply to give some small help to one young person trying to break out of poverty and it just so happened that the student chosen for me was Wittaya.

I sent off the first payment and some time later received a long letter from him, written in Thai but with an English translation from the Foundation. He explained that when lack of money had forced him to stop studying, he had left Bangkok and travelled to more remote parts of Thailand. The trip had obviously been a real eye-opener. He wrote:

> *I got a lot of experiences to answer my questions. The best experience I had was to be an assistant teacher to the hill tribe children in the north of Thailand. These children are not different from the children of the towns. Children everywhere are like flowers which are just coming into bloom.*
>
> *I concluded that I had to come back to Bangkok to further my study, to get more knowledge and a degree which is acceptable in today's Thai culture. I lack knowledge — that's why I decided to further my studies.*

The Foundation encouraged sponsors to write to their students but I never did. In fact, I began to feel uneasy about

77

our relationship. Twice a year Wittaya sent short but highly respectful notes, reporting on how his studies were going and expressing his gratitude for my support, but frankly I could well afford the money and felt slightly embarrassed by his profusion of thanks.

Even when he wrote that he would like to receive letters from me and to know about my country I still didn't respond. Now, I wonder why not. Was it just uneasiness about the unequal nature of the relationship? Was I trying to keep him at arm's length and, if so, why? Was it just laziness? I don't know, but I certainly regret not allowing the relationship to grow into something stronger and more rewarding for both of us.

Although I didn't write to Wittaya, I did once visit him during a trip to Bangkok. It was the briefest of encounters. We met at the Foundation, went on to his home, exchanged small gifts and, with one of the Foundation's staff acting as translator, had a rather stilted conversation. Then we said goodbye and returned to a six-monthly exchange of sponsorship cheques and letters of thanks.

By 1994 Wittaya was approaching the end of his studies and wrote to say that he hoped to work in the countryside 'as I know there are few people interested to develop the area.' That was the last time I heard from him. The following year the Foundation said he no longer needed support and asked me instead to help a girl at a vocational college. I didn't even know for sure whether Wittaya had graduated. It was an unsatisfactory end to what had been a rather unsatisfactory and uneasy relationship.

So in 1997 I went back to Bangkok, to find out what had happened and to meet Wittaya again — this time not as sponsor to student, but as man to man.

The Search Begins

I didn't expect to stay for more than a few days. The Duang Prateep Foundation had given me a contact number for Wittaya and it seemed the search would be straightforward — which only goes to show how wrong you can be. The search — or, rather, the wait — for Wittaya became a frustrating trail of inadequate information and long delays, a lesson in patience and the ways of Asia.

The first call signalled trouble. A friend at the Foundation frowned as she put down the phone.

'That was his grandmother,' she explained. 'She says Wittaya has gone up-country and she doesn't know where he is or when he'll be back.'

I walked to Chulalongkorn University, the most renowned and prestigious institute of learning in Thailand, hoping to find a student who could act as my interpreter, so that I could go to Wittaya's home and speak to someone face to face. It was the Saturday morning before mid-term exams and the campus was almost deserted, but there were four students in the English Club and one of them was eager to help. His name was Songphon Mungkongsujarit.

'Very long, isn't it?' he laughed as he spelled it out. 'But you can call me Sunny.'

Sunny was in his final year of a course in electrical engineering and hoping for a scholarship to go overseas to get a Masters degree. He was Thai Chinese from an upper middle-class family and had never set foot in Klong Toey but was intrigued to find out whether the stories of squalid living conditions and rampant crime were really true.

'Just studying pure engineering is useless,' he said. 'I must open my vision.'

Sunny called Wittaya's home and managed to speak to his wife, Somchit, who agreed to meet us early the next morning.

She gave instructions on how to get to the family home in Klong Toey — turn left in front of the school, turn right when you get to the wall of the port, then take the third lane on the right and walk until you see a house on the right with a blue gate.

It was a two-storey building with a concrete floor, wooden walls and a tin roof, hemmed in by similar homes on either side and opening onto a concrete alley which was barely wide enough for two people to pass. We sat downstairs in a large room which had clearly been much lived in. On the walls were a family photograph, a picture of the King and Queen and a large poster of a pop group. An electric fan silently freshened the warm morning air.

Wittaya's mother, Mrs. Buitsak, sat on the floor, a plump, smiling woman in a cotton blouse and skirt, with gold earrings and a gold bracelet. Somchit was tall and slim, dressed simply in a T-shirt and sarong, and Vichit, Wittaya's strong, boisterous four-year-old son, was playing on the floor stark naked.

Somchit explained that for the past year Wittaya had been working for a construction company in Krabi, almost one thousand kilometres away in the south of Thailand. He came home for only a couple of days each month and she didn't expect to see him again for three weeks. No, she didn't have a contact number for him and simply waited for him to call. She thought he would probably call again in two or three days' time and said she would tell him that we wanted to see him.

Mrs. Buitsak was all smiles but Somchit was clearly suspicious of this stranger come searching for her husband. She was polite and friendly but reticent. She told us that she and Wittaya had met at a party when they were students. She confirmed that they had both graduated, told us that she worked as a secretary for a multinational company and that she was about to study for a Masters degree. But that was about it.

She went upstairs and found a large photograph of Wittaya receiving his degree from Crown Prince Maha Vajiralongkorn. Mrs. Buitsak showed the picture to Vichit, probably for the umpteenth time, and said she had been so proud of Wittaya on that day that she had cried. Her little grandson, grasping the moral of the story, burst into the chorus of a popular Thai rap song:

> *Torn lek lek, mai rian nang seu,*
> *Thor khun mar, tong kut rong taow!*

If you don't study hard when you're young, you'll only be able to polish shoes when you grow up!

We said our goodbyes and left. I wondered briefly about going down to Krabi and trying to find Wittaya there but decided against it. Krabi was only a temporary workplace. Klong Toey was home.

There was only one thing to do. Await Wittaya's return.

The Flame of Enlightenment

One day, outside the swanky World Trade Centre, I met a young man called Lek, who was studying English in order to advance from being a hotel waiter to working as a receptionist. He asked what I was doing in Bangkok and when I mentioned Klong Toey he frowned. 'People in Klong Toey no good,' he said, placing his fist below his nose and snorting in imitation of a glue sniffer. Then he tapped his finger on the side of his head. 'Bad people,' he said. 'Crazy.'

The name *Klong Toey* means a canal fringed with pandanus trees. Slender pandanus leaves are used in flower arrangements

and to add fragrance in cooking, but there was nothing elegant or fragrant about Klong Toey, no pandanus trees in sight. It was a just a big city slum, a sweltering, sprawling maze of huts, many of them squeezed between the Port of Bangkok to the south and an expressway and a railway line to the north. The slum was so large that it was divided into twenty-four communities. In some, such as the one in which Wittaya and his family lived, the houses were built on dry land with solid materials, but in the worst areas they were just ramshackle huts, odd bits of wood and metal hammered together, standing on stilts in pools of stagnant water and linked by a vast network of narrow crisscrossing paths.

Most of the people in Klong Toey earned meagre money as labourers at the port or as vendors, and the average family income was about 6,000 *baht* or 150 dollars per month. There was the usual depressing catalogue of problems that beset poor people in large cities at the end of the twentieth century. Children as young as seven sniffed glue. Drug abuse was rampant and the sharing of needles had spread HIV. Drug dealers operated quite openly.

'Even small children know which house to go to,' said one social worker. 'It's as easy as buying toffees or sweets.'

Yet in the middle of this notorious slum lived one of Thailand's most famous and most respected women, Prateep Ungsongtham, founder of the Duang Prateep Foundation, the organization which had first brought Wittaya and me together.

As a teenager, scraping rust from ships in the port, Prateep had noticed that her fellow labourers often missed work because they had nobody to look after their children. She had opened an informal — and illegal — school in her home, charging one *baht* per child per day, and was soon caring for one hundred children. The school became the focal point of the community. Prateep survived attempts to evict her, and her success made other residents realize that they too had rights. In 1978, when she was just twenty-six, she won Asia's version of the Nobel Prize, the Ramon Magsaysay Award, and used her prize money to launch the Duang Prateep Foundation — literally, the Flame of Enlightenment Foundation.

Twenty years on, Prateep almost ran into her office for our early morning meeting, elegantly dressed and looking for all the world like a bustling businesswoman. Only a red AIDS ribbon in her lapel suggested someone more interested in people than profits.

'I'm sorry I'm fifteen minutes late,' she said, speaking quickly and glancing at her watch. 'No, seventeen minutes. Sorry, sorry.'

I was the first engagement of another busy day. Her diary included a meeting with officials about setting up a fire station in Klong Toey, greeting a party of visiting schoolgirls, hosting a photographer from the United Nations Drug Control Programme, attending a ceremony at a kindergarten to mark the Buddhist Khao Phansaa festival and planning an anti-drugs mini marathon.

Prateep lived with her husband and two sons in a small house barely fifty metres from the Foundation. I wondered why, being so aware of the slum's problems, she still chose to live there.

She burst out laughing. 'I have no money,' she said, 'no money to go anywhere!'

Then, becoming more serious, she said that when she won the Magsaysay Award in 1978 the money had been enough to buy four townhouses in Bangkok and she had thought for a moment about buying one for herself.

'But another thought coming in — if I take the money and buy a townhouse, people in the community will look at me and say oh, I am selfish, just trying to find a way to escape the problem by myself, so I decide to put the money to start the Foundation.'

Then, another burst of laughter.

'You know, in those days one town house was — you know how much? One hundred thousand *baht*. Today, five million!'

Then, becoming serious again, 'But if compared to the work of the Foundation, that is nothing, could not be compared.'

I wondered whether, after living in Klong Toey all her life, Prateep felt she knew the place and its people inside out or whether slum life could still surprise her. Oh, she said, she could still be shocked. Just a few days before she had met a young handicapped boy outside her house, his head covered in scabs. She had swung into action, first tracking down the boy's grandmother and then discovering that his father was one of her former students. The man's wife had run away and left him with four young children, but the basic problem, concluded Prateep, was poverty.

'I know my student,' she said. 'He's not very clever, but he's not stupid. He works very hard but his wages are very low and when one member of the family has a complication — like this boy now — we have no system to support them.'

The previous evening after work Prateep had gone out to buy the boy some clean clothes, and she was planning to register him as a handicapped person, so that his family could receive 500 *baht* per month from the government. He would have to be educated and, if no other facilities were available, she would admit him to the Foundation's own kindergarten, just across the road from her office.

'Come,' she said, 'I'd like you to meet him.'

We walked out into the maze of houses and small stores and Prateep soon spotted the boy's brother. She asked him to fetch the boy, and a couple of minutes later, along one of the slum's narrow paths, the two of them walked towards us.

Am was four years old. He could not walk steadily and held the hand of his older brother. There were scabs all over his scalp, but what really struck me was how dirty he was. There was a thick black grime under his fingernails and the risk of further infection to his scabs was horribly obvious.

In addition to his physical problems, he seemed to be mildly mentally handicapped.

Prateep squatted down and talked to him, her peach-coloured jacket sweeping the dirty pathway.

'You ask me why I stay in the slum,' said Prateep. 'This is why. Because I can get the information. When I go to the market, I meet so many people. Every Saturday I join with the community people for night patrol, so that I can see. If I don't stay in Klong Toey, I don't know.'

She conceded that the slum was not the ideal place for her own sons to grow up. In fact, she said, it was worse now than it had been when she was a child. In her early years the only drug addicts in Klong Toey were old opium addicts, but now there was widespread abuse of heroin and amphetamines and many people sniffed glue.

'What do you think your boys learn from growing up in Klong Toey?' I asked.

'To be a fighter. Not physical fight, but my sons have ideas and reasons, and even when we quarrel with each other they can find very good reasons against me,' she said.

But were conditions in Klong Toey really worse now than when she was a girl? Wittaya's mother said things had improved enormously over the twenty years she had been living there.

'If housing, pathways, water and electricity, yes, she is totally right,' said Prateep. 'But look at the chemical explosions in the port, seven or eight hurting this community, and now they are going to build an even bigger chemical store. How many fires we have, how many drug addicts we have?'

So which of Klong Toey's many problems was the most serious? Which worried her most? Was it the overcrowding, the poor sanitation, lack of hygiene, the threat of fires and chemical explosions, loan sharking, crime, drugs, poverty, inadequate education? What?

She thought for a time and then surprised me with her answer.

'Destroying community leaders,' she said.

Two forces, she explained, had vested interests in undermining strong community organizations and good leaders. The first was the Port Authority, which wanted to reclaim land at

Klong Toey and knew that resistance by strong communities would make its task infinitely more difficult. The second force were the gangsters who operated in the slum and whose businesses, such as drug dealing, were threatened by community education and community spirit. These two forces, Prateep said, tried every means to bring down good community leaders.

'Every time when any good movement happens they will try to find some weak point and set up bad rumours,' she said. 'So this worries me most. In the long run, it is weakening the community.'

Sometimes the struggles also weakened Prateep. One of Thailand's biggest drug dealers was based in Klong Toey and such powerful criminals were threatened by her work. In a quiet moment she admitted that over the past couple of years the strain had begun to tell and she felt that she had aged quickly. There had been many death threats.

'They want to kill me,' she said.

'Do you take the threats seriously?'

'Yes. I don't mind in the daytime, but when they come to my house in the night I do feel a little bit scared.' Then she laughed again. 'But if I am still breathing, I keep fighting!'

The Duang Prateep Foundation had been started to provide education for chil-

dren in Klong Toey, but had grown to become a large agency running a wide range of services — community development programmes, AIDS prevention, a children's art club, rehabilitation of young drug addicts, services for the elderly, a school for children with impaired hearing, emergency as-

sistance, a young women's project, a credit union and a rural relocation programme for people who wanted to leave Bangkok and return to the countryside. It had even acquired a couple of secondhand fire engines and formed its own team of volunteer firefighters.

'It is not the right way, to just only do education,' said Prateep. 'We have to find some way to voice our concerns about the way of development.'

'So you're no longer a teacher,' I said. 'You've become a politician.'

For the first and only time in our conversation, her face became stern.

'No. I am not a politician,' she said emphatically. 'I am a social worker, a social development worker. I have to use the politics to help the people and to prevent more people from suffering, but I am not a politician. No, no.'

Despite diversifying its services, the Foundation's primary focus was still education, with fifteen slum kindergartens

around Bangkok and more than two thousand five hundred students being sponsored.

'Education is the most important part,' said Prateep, 'but we should not think that education is only classroom and children. We should include the parents, the community, community leaders, help them to think that if we want our children to get a good education then what kind of environment we should create. If the community is good, even if the children have problem they could not turn bad.'

'Eh!' she said in exasperation. 'I cannot explain well enough in English.'

'No, you're very clear, but let me turn it around. If the community is bad, is it impossible for the children to turn out good?'

'Everyone when they are first born is same same, but most children can be influenced by their environment, the way of the parents and the community surrounding them,' she said.

Another smile broke across her face.

'But even if the environment is bad, some will be good — like me!' Peals of laughter.

We went outside again to take some more photos. After so many years in the limelight, Prateep was completely at ease before the camera.

In the street, two young men were shouting loudly, drawing attention to themselves, but when one of them spotted Prateep he immediately fell silent and came to stand in front of her with his head bowed.

'Drug addict,' she explained.

She checked his arms for needle marks. There was none, but Prateep was not fooled.

'He just inject in some other part,' she said.

She talked to the young man for a while and suggested he join the Foundation's New Life programme, which took young people away from Klong Toey to be rehabilitated on a farm in the southern province of Chumphon. The man was clearly drugged and could scarcely focus as he tried to answer. He said he would think about it in two or three days' time.

'Why wait?' she said. 'Come today.'

The man prevaricated again, warning that he might not get along with the staff at Chumphon.

'If you don't like it, I'll bring you back here,' said Prateep. 'I give you my promise.'

She pulled the man's head to her shoulder, stroked his hair and gave him a few words of advice. Then, after they parted, she turned to me and said glumly that he would never join her programme. She had been trying to help him for three years without success. If the police arrested him, at least he would be put into a rehabilitation programme, but they couldn't be bothered. He was just one Klong Toey addict, one among hundreds.

We walked back to the office, passing a gaunt man in a grey shirt and shorts who was smiling vacantly, as high as a kite.

'Sniffing glue,' said Prateep.

We had not been in the street for ten minutes, yet in that short time we had, without looking for them, met two young drug addicts and a glue sniffer — and all this in the most prosperous and well-established part of Klong Toey.

There remained much darkness for the flame of enlightenment to dispel.

Culture and Community

Meanwhile, I waited for Wittaya.

Sunny called Somchit every couple of days to see if there was any news but never got a clear answer. One evening he spoke to Wittaya's father who said that, maybe, his son would return the following week.

'But what does that word "maybe" mean?' asked Sunny, exasperated.

We had no idea whether Wittaya would return the next day, next week or next month. In fact, I began to wonder if he would ever come back, but on reflection the lack of information from his family was understandable. A tall pink foreigner had suddenly arrived at their home and started asking all sorts of personal questions. Why was he so interested in Wittaya? It made no sense, all this talk about a book. Better be careful. Talk to Wittaya when he came home. Anyway, what did it matter which day Wittaya would return to Bangkok? He would return when he returned.

There was nothing I could do. Except wait.

Not that waiting was any great hardship amidst the charms of Bangkok. Whenever the heat and pollution began to feel oppressive, a sudden splash of colour, a fragrance, a taste, a graceful gesture or a detail of design would lighten my mood. I would be walking along a busy street, choking on vehicle fumes, and suddenly catch sight of sunshine glinting on a temple roof or drops of water glistening on a mound of freshly picked orchids. Or, passing a building site, spot amongst the mess of rubble and scaffolding a spirit house decorated with fresh *puang malai*, little garlands of

white jasmine, yellow marigolds and red rosebuds. In a garden in the red-light district of Patpong, a group of musicians sat on a low teak table under a mango tree and played tinkling traditional music, their notes lingering in the air like wisps of smoke from incense.

The days slipped slowly by.

King Bhumibol went to Wat Phra Keow and changed the clothes on the Emerald Buddha in preparation for the rainy season, and that very day a huge black storm cloud formed over Bangkok and the first rains fell. The *baht* fell, too, losing almost a quarter of its value, bad news for poor people who would soon find imported items soaring in cost.

One morning Sunny and I turned off at random down a narrow pathway to explore a different section of Klong Toey, what you might call a middle-class slum neighbourhood. Again, delicate details drew my eyes away from the squalor — a little shrine wedged between two huts and decked with fresh flowers; a row of orchids hanging over a porch; a cage of brightly coloured birds outside a rice store.

Prateep had said that ten major fires in Klong Toey in recent years had left more than twenty-five thousand people homeless, and walking down between the densely packed huts the potential for disaster was obvious. No fire engine could possibly enter those narrow lanes, yet dangerous chemicals were stored just a stone's throw away, behind the port wall.

A woman, dripping with sweat, pushed past us with a heavy barrow of ice; an old man sat cross-legged on a wooden platform in front of his hut, about to eat a fried fish; two young men lolled on a small balcony, chatting; many mothers were washing clothes in large bowls of suds; the owner of a small electrical repair store was examining the innards of a video player; an old woman sat in the doorway of her home, smoking a hand rolled cigarette.

We meandered along in no particular direction, exchanging greetings and smiles with people we passed, observing, chatting, comparing impressions, and then suddenly we emerged on to a patch of open ground where some fifty people were clearing rubbish to make way for a children's playground. It was a completely accidental discovery and the most extraordinary sight.

The area was about half the size of a football pitch and was bisected by a concrete path. On one side of the path was a thick platform of rotting garbage, almost waist high, and residents with rakes were standing on and around the platform, tugging the garbage into large wicker baskets for others to drag away.

Most of the workers were men but there were women too and even some children helping around the edges. One middle-aged man was so drunk that he could scarcely coordinate his movements, but even he had a rake and was tearing  wildly at the mound of putrid waste. The stench was foul and all the workers wore cotton masks over their mouths and noses.

On the other side of the path, the area being cleared was not land but water. Many houses in this part of Klong Toey were built on stilts above stinking, stagnant pools. The water had been poisoned and turned a vile black by years of pollution, although on the surface there was a rich growth of plants. In one corner, garbage and weeds had formed such a thick crust that a man was able to stand on it. Workers along the path were raking in all the rubbish they could reach, and a high pressure water pump which was usually used for firefighting had been brought in to loosen the larger clusters of plants and rubbish.

I began to take photographs, unable to resist a shot of an immaculate spirit house decorated with many fresh *puang malai*, the pure white jasmine flowers contrasting with the blackness of the pool.

Then, out of the corner of my eye, I noticed something moving and realized to my horror that a small boy was actually in the water, pulling at the most stubborn bits of rubbish. He was swimming slowly through the blackness, dragging a raft of garbage and plants behind him, and when his load became too heavy, a worker on the path stretched out a rake and the boy clung on to the prongs and was dragged to the side of the pool. He moved a sheet of corrugated iron, charred timbers from a hut fire, an old football, plastic sandals, clumps of plants and polystyrene boxes — and all the time he was swimming in poisonous filth.

I couldn't take my eyes off him and squatted down beside

the pool, taking photographs, grimacing and cursing quietly as the black water lapped at his lips. Years before in Manila and Calcutta I had met families who made a living by scavenging on municipal dumps, hardworking and eagle eyed people who picked through the garbage as soon as it was dumped

94

from a truck, knowing exactly what they were looking for. That was not a pretty sight in tropical heat and a haze of flies or, worse, during the monsoon, when the rains turned the top layer of the dump to liquid. Yet I had never seen anything so repulsive as watching this little lad swimming in the filth of Klong Toey.

Eventually he clambered out, dragging himself across the piles of debris he had helped to retrieve. Despite the scorching heat, he was shivering. He walked down the path and began to wash,

scooping clean water from a large pot and pouring it over himself. He had no soap and it took a while to get rid of all the rubbish that had stuck to him.

'How old are you?' I asked.

'Eleven.'

'And what's your name?'

'Ton.'

'Why did you go into the water?'

'Someone told me to.'

'Weren't you worried about how dirty it was?'

'No.' A long pause. 'But now I feel not comfortable.'

He walked off down the path towards his home, scratching himself furiously. There was a large open cut on his left leg.

Seeing Ton in the water had been so repulsive, so shocking, that I had ignored the rest of the clearance, but after he had gone I realized that revulsion had to be tempered by admiration. It was actually an impressive and well-organized community effort. The residents were all working as volunteers, giving up Sunday, their one free day, to clear the area. Everyone had been equipped with a mask and a rake, and two girls walked around the site dispensing glasses of iced water. Loudspeakers called on other residents to come out and join the effort and announced the various organizations and individuals who had contributed to the cost of the new playground. Someone had donated rice to feed the volunteers.

I wondered what Sunny made of it all.

'Of course, the place is disgusting,' he said, 'but when I see the people working together to help themselves — that impresses me a lot. When people have community spirit, they can fight for anything.'

We were introduced to Plaeng Sridanoi, doyen of Klong Toey community workers, who had moved to the slum forty years earlier. I asked whether most children were now able to study and find jobs which allowed them to move away, and Mr. Sridanoi said it all depended on education. Some children were fine, but others from very poor families could only afford to study for nine years of compulsory education and then fell in with 'bad people'.

'We are trying to protect them from drugs and crime,' he said. 'Maybe this day is an example. We are trying to build a playground so that they have somewhere to play sport and not get involved with drugs.'

As we sat beside the path talking to Mr. Sridanoi, a boy came by on an old pink bicycle. It was Ton. Half an hour after climbing out of the pool, he was dried and dressed and had stopped scratching. His morning's work was over. No big deal. Just another day in Klong Toey.

I went back to my room at the YMCA and stood for a long time in a hot shower.

As Firm as a Mountain

And still I waited for Wittaya.

One week became two, two became three, three would soon become four. In a couple more days I would need to go to the Immigration Department and ask for an extension of stay. The wait began to seem like a huge waste of time, a rather ridiculous obsession. I didn't even know Wittaya Buitsak. Suppose he turned out to be a thoroughly unpleasant character. What a disappointment that would be.

Then, late one evening, Sunny called in great excitement.

'I have the good news!' he said. 'Wittaya is right now here in Bangkok. He can see you tomorrow morning.'

'Great!' I said.

A pause at the other end of the line.

'But I am not free,' said Sunny. 'I have classes tomorrow morning.'

Poor Sunny! After all his help and enthusiasm, he never did meet Wittaya, but we couldn't let this chance of a meeting slip and so a friend agreed at short notice to stand in as translator.

Wittaya walked up to me the following morning, smiling gently, his hands placed together as if in prayer, making a respectful *wai* of greeting. Five years on and the boy had become a man. I noticed his eyes, sunk deep in his head, and his large, strong hands, but what struck me most forcibly, even in those first few minutes, was how self-possessed he was. In a very Thai way, without a hint of loudness or arrogance, he took charge of the situation. A man to have beside you in a crisis, calm, steady, strong.

I apologized for having troubled his family with so many calls.

'Mai pen rai, mai pen rai,' he said with a smile, 'never mind.'

We began to make up for lost time.

Wittaya explained that he had graduated from college two years earlier with a degree in mass communications, but had then joined his father's small business, maintaining pipelines for an international oil company. Later he had joined a larger company as a purchasing officer and was now working on the construction of a new airport in Krabi, in charge of stock control and with three workmen reporting to him.

He liked Krabi, didn't miss Bangkok and didn't mind the long drive home at the end of each month, but he felt restless in the seething city and often took himself off to the forests of Ratchaburi, to walk, camp and hunt wild birds for a couple of days. Young Thai men traditionally spend a few weeks or months as monks, making merit for their families. Wittaya had not yet done this but said, 'When I am in the forest I feel more calm than people who have been a monk.'

'How often do you escape to the forest?' I asked. 'Once a month? Once a year?'

'Once a month,' he said, adding with a smile, 'if twice a month is possible, it's better.'

But why, after studying mass communications, had he gone into the construction business? Well, he said, it was a matter of money and opportunity. You needed connections to succeed in the media, but construction was different and he hoped to start his own company. He had been in Krabi for almost a year and reckoned he needed three or four more years' experience before setting up on his own.

'Do you really think it will be possible to start your own company?' I asked.

'Possible,' he said, speaking softly but with a firmness and confidence that left no doubt about his determination.

After we had been talking for an hour or so, I asked him to cast his mind back to his childhood in Klong Toey. Did he agree with his mother that living conditions in the slum had improved over the years, or was Prateep right in saying that things had deteriorated?

The atmosphere between us suddenly changed. Wittaya paused, thought for a moment and then, instead of answering my question, turned to my friend.

'I want to ask Chris about his book,' he said seriously. 'I want to know what about the effect for Thailand.'

My friend turned and translated Wittaya's concern. 'He is a little bit worried, a little bit confused,' he explained. 'Me, too.'

Their concern was that I might use their words to project a negative image of Thailand, for they had learned through sad experience that foreigners didn't always understand or respect the dignity of the Kingdom. I said that most people overseas had never been to Thailand and that many of those who did come as tourists didn't get beyond the Grand Palace, the floating market and the seedy bars of Patpong. I hoped simply to show another side of Bangkok life and to tell part of the story of one of the city's six million people.

Wittaya accepted this explanation but said that he was not an open man. He liked to keep to himself. If another man got too much information about his life, he said, that man would own his life. Anyway, he was not a successful man — for instance, he knew little about agriculture.

'He says that anything he tells you from his knowledge or from his experience or from his heart is just coming from a small man in society,' said my friend. 'He cannot speak for other people.'

After an assurance that I was not seeking to portray him as a hero or as a spokesman, Wittaya said, 'Okay, I'll answer your questions. Firstly, because you helped me in the past and, secondly, if I can help you to reflect the true picture of our country I will feel good.' The decision of a polite, dignified, uncompromising man.

Wittaya's sharpest early memories of Klong Toey were of the excitement of walking through the slum on rickety boardwalks which spanned the pools of filthy water and having to balance carefully to avoid falling in. The physical environment today was much, much better.

'Surely my son's prospects will be better than mine,' he said. 'When I was four years old, my parents' vision for me was very different from my vision now for my son. I have a wider vision than they did. I know about the importance of education.'

Prateep had said that growing up in Klong Toey was teaching her sons to be fighters. What, I wondered, had it taught Wittaya?

He thought for a while in silence, tapping the table top, regarding me steadily. The question implied that Klong Toey was specially terrible and he wasn't going to allow such an inference to pass unchallenged.

'Sure, when I was in college and my friends found out that I was from this area they said, 'Wow, you're from slum Klong Toey.' But not everyone from Klong Toey is bad, you know. There are good people from this area as well.'

Outsiders saw only the negative side of the slum and ignored the important fact that Klong Toey was a place where people without much money could rent a cheap space to live right in the centre of the city.

'Mind you,' he added, 'the one thing that Klong Toey people are afraid of is fire. Deep in their hearts they are afraid of it, and so if they can find a way to leave Klong Toey they will.'

'Do you think you will move?'

'Sure.'

He thought for a moment and then qualified his answer. If he could be certain that his family home wouldn't be cleared by the Port Authority and if the danger of fire could be reduced, then he would stay. Klong Toey was home, the place where he had grown up.

Mind you, growing up had been a painful business, particularly in his teenaged years when his relationship with his father had been very stormy.

'He wanted me to come home at the same time every day,' he said. 'I said to him: "You raise me like a girl, not like a boy. I want adventure."'

Even as a man, Wittaya was still searing in his criticism of the way in which his parents had brought him up, at one point saying, 'I would hate myself if I raised my son as I was raised by my parents.' Yet there was not a trace of bitterness in his judgement and he was scrupulous to exonerate his parents from blame and to stress that old wounds had healed.

'It's not my parents' fault,' he said. 'Farm people think only about agriculture, they know only what time to plant, what time to harvest. They don't think about the future, they

101

just think about where to get food for the next meal.'

The angry teenager had taken himself north to Chiang Mai, working as a volunteer on a forestry project, giving his labour in return for food and a place to sleep, learning about the problems of Thailand's hill tribes. Eventually, as he had told me in that first letter eight years earlier, he had met a teacher and helped to teach tribal children.

'I found that some people were less fortunate than me, some people were poorer than me, they couldn't even read or have enough food to eat,' he said. 'They deserved help from other people more than I did. So I asked the teacher what I could do to help them and he asked me a good question — "What did you graduate in?" At that time I hadn't graduated in anything, so his question made me think that I should come back to Bangkok and complete my education. At that time I had only a technician's vocabulary.'

So Wittaya had returned to Bangkok and resumed his studies. At precisely the point at which many Klong Toey youngsters were snared by a web of drugs and crime, Wittaya had matured and forged the values and beliefs which still guided his thinking as an adult.

'I still haven't found myself very clearly,' he said frankly. 'I still have a dream to help the hill tribe people, but in my present situation I have restrictions. I have a wife and a son. If I leave my family now and go back to work in the mountains — well, in my deep heart I don't feel it would be the right thing to do. But I still have the intention to help.'

In fact, he had more than an intention. He had a long-term plan to be successful in his work and then to move back to Chiang Mai, to get a Masters degree in agriculture and to have his own farm. There, living in a rural community, he would get to know people's problems and be able to talk to them directly. He would hire poor people to work his land.

'I think that is a very close and direct way to help people,' he said.

This was not naive idealism but the considered aspiration of a mature and sensible man, someone who was determined to discharge his responsibilities as a husband and father but who at the same time wanted to help other people. His motivation to help sprang mainly from his experience in the mountains but also, he said, from the fact that he had been given financial assistance during his education.

'The foundation helped me to receive so that I know also how to give,' he said.

'What dreams do you have for your son?' I asked.

'Well, I don't expect that he will be in this occupation or that occupation. He can choose for himself. As a father, I will be a support to him. My son makes a decision to walk. If he falls, I'll bring him back up again, but I won't hold him while he walks, or walk instead of him.

'The important difference is that now I am a father I'm ready to really hear my son, to accept him and to understand him. When I was a boy I didn't have such a person. I am my son's best friend. Now he is only four years old so he doesn't have many questions, but when he grows up I am ready to answer his questions. I will compensate for the things which I lacked when I was a boy.'

However, the father who had fought so hard to become himself knew that his son would also have to struggle.

'I have a dream for him,' he said, 'but it depends on him to work hard for himself. As far as I can, I will offer him everything he needs — food, education, whatever — but the future depends on my son.'

After we had been talking for a long time, I asked Wittaya whether he would mind if I took some photographs of him as he spoke.

'Why?' he asked.

'Because it will help readers to relate to your story if they can see pictures of you and your family.'

'Are they essential for you?'

I considered.

'Well, no,' I said, 'I can't say that they're essential. They would be very helpful, but only if you are happy for me to use them.'

We talked about this for some time and eventually I suggested three photos — the one of Wittaya receiving his degree, one of him now and one of him with his son. He acknowledged that the degree photograph would show that he had successfully completed his formal education and so gave me a copy. He allowed me to photograph him as we spoke, but he didn't want Vichit to be pictured in an article about him.

'Vichit will have his own life,' he said.

What a beautiful, respectful thing for a man to say of his four-year-old son.

I began to take photos, but whereas Prateep had positively performed for the camera, Wittaya was unsettled by it. The nervous, diffident character showing through the lens bore no resemblance to the self-assured man chatting beside me. So I stopped. Perhaps one lucky shot had captured a fair likeness. If not, the picture would have to be painted in words.

I said to him, 'You've already told me that you don't regard yourself as a successful man, but are you a contented man? You're only twenty-eight and still have most of your life in front of you, but how do you assess your life so far?'

'Right now I am content,' he said. 'I feel quite content that I have a Bachelor's degree and that I passed the difficult turning point when I was a teenager without getting into trouble. So far, so good.'

There was no arrogance or complacency in his assessment. It was just typically Wittaya — a fair and realistic appraisal by a quiet, serious man who at times during our conversation seemed almost to be an observer of his own life, sounding more like a coach than a player, talking about himself with a remarkable objectivity and honesty.

We talked and talked over two days. I asked endless questions and he recalled memories which were sometimes painful, but there were also times, over lunch or crawling through the traffic in his pick-up truck, when we chatted more generally, about everything from the Karen rebels in Burma to our favourite movies.

Eight years on, Wittaya and I became friends.

He said he enjoyed our conversations because we talked about things he could rarely discuss and he had to use his brain to think about my questions. I said that I had learned much from his answers.

'I think that everybody has a good side and a bad side,' said Wittaya. 'I'm not the best and I'm not the worst. I'm in the middle. I won't oppress people, won't take advantage of other people, but at the same time I won't let other people take advantage of me.'

I recalled the words of a younger, greener Wittaya, in that first letter to me eight years earlier.

I like mountains and forests. The mountain gives me a sense of security, determination and the greatness of nature. Maybe this is the place which forms my personality. It makes me become a determined person — that is, whatever I do, I'll do it with my whole spirit and whole strength until I succeed. Never give up. As firm as a mountain.

CHAPTER 5

India, Calcutta

Future Hope

A City of Contrasts

A battered old Ambassador taxi had brought me from the airport to the heart of Calcutta, spluttering through the night along unlit roads, splashing through enormous puddles, scattering unwary pedestrians and delivering me finally into the compound of Queen's Mansions, where it shuddered to a halt.

I walked into the darkened building. The lift gates were chained and padlocked and the three attendants were sound asleep in the lobby. Not having the heart to wake them, I began to heave my bags up the stairs. The walls were stained with spits of betel nut juice and the ceiling was strewn with black cobwebs as thick as fingers, but up on the fourth floor the Bengal Chambers guesthouse was clean and friendly. I was shown to an enormous room with two beds, two large wardrobes, a desk, a coffee table, a sofa, four chairs and acres of space to spare. The ceiling was high enough to accommodate a two-storey house, and there was a large balcony with two cane chairs, once bright red but long since blackened by grime from the street below. The toilet flushed on impulse rather than to instruction and the bathroom was the sort of place where you just poured a bucket of water over your head and ran for the door, but otherwise everything was fine.

Most of the staff were old men and one of them, Ali, a cheerful fellow with a trim silver moustache and grey hair sprouting from his ears, was put in charge of me. He served breakfast in the dining room in a waiter's white uniform and then reappeared in my room ten minutes later, wearing a brown outfit and ready to clean. He called me 'Master' and served salt with a tiny silver spoon. At sundown he appeared in the room with a pot of hot tea, served on a tray with a delicate china cup and two sweet biscuits. It was all very English, a little old-fashioned, rather nice.

Calcutta was founded by the British in 1690 and in 1858 became the capital of India, but when in 1911 the British had a

change of heart and moved the capital to Delhi, the fabric of Calcutta began to fade. By the time of my arrival, Queen's Mansions, once a most desirable address, was degenerating into a warren of cheap guesthouses, dark apartments and restaurant kitchens. The exterior of the building was crumbling and, while the good lady proprietors of the Bengal Chambers tried their best to maintain standards, their landlords seemed resigned to decay.

Calcutta in its heyday must have been a magnificent sight,

constructed on the grandest scale, dubbed the City of Palaces and second only to London among the cities of the British Empire. Even in 1997, half a century after the British departed, the architecture remained colonial and at every turn there were teasing reminders of how things used to be. A sign reading 'Calcutta Kennel Club (Est'd 1906)' evoked images of colonial ladies gathering to admire each other's lap dogs and share the latest gossip from Sussex and Kent. I looked in vain for impressive new Indian buildings but found instead yet more splendid old colonial edifices being slowly smothered by tropical creepers and decaying to the march of time. It was like walking through an architectural mortuary.

The pollution from vehicle fumes was horrific. The Maidan, a vast parkland in the heart of the city, used to be Calcutta's lungs, but now during the evening rush hour the air was blue with fumes. This wasn't the sort of dirt which could be removed with a quick sluice from the Bengal Chambers' bucket. It seemed to seep into the very pores of my skin and I felt myself turning grey. After a few hours on the streets, my fair eyebrows turned to streaks of charcoal. There were black specks in my spittle.

Yet, despite its pollution and its hopelessly inadequate infrastructure, despite the ghastly living conditions endured by so many of its people and a hideously inhospitable climate, it was good to be back in Calcutta. If the buildings were ever cleaned they would probably fall down and if the city ever stopped to draw breath it would surely die, but the whole point about Calcutta is that it *doesn't* stop to draw breath. It has an incredible energy and its people have a flair for living, getting on with their lives in defiance of the physical problems. The international image of people lying helplessly in the streets and waiting to be

picked up by the Missionaries of Charity couldn't be further from the truth. Calcutta is a cauldron of energy, a reminder of how tough, how creative and how cheerful the human spirit can be. Tim Grandage, an old friend from Hong Kong, had lived there for more than ten years and I asked him how he felt about the place.

'Very ambivalent,' he said. 'I absolutely love it most of the time, but some of the time I hate it. But that's Calcutta. It's a city of contrasts. You'll never have much in the middle.'

At the bottom of the city's heap of twelve million people are those who live on the streets, hundreds of thousands of them, from newborn babies to the ancient and dying. Calcutta is a magnet, drawing to itself people with one-way tickets from all over eastern India and Bangladesh. They come expecting the streets to be paved with gold but find instead that they are paved with people.

Nobody knows how many of Calcutta's street people are children but estimates are in the hundreds of thousands. Some are with their families but many are completely alone, on the run from broken homes and violent fathers. They are pretty tough characters, survivors in a loveless world, but they are not being educated and their values are the law of the jungle. Worst of all, they are unloved.

An agency called Future Hope was helping these street children, caring for more than eighty youngsters in four homes in the south of Calcutta. The homes were for children who really wanted to come off the streets, turn their lives around and make a new start, and, even though such a transformation takes years to effect and Future Hope was still young, some forty young people had already graduated and moved on to find jobs and live independently in the community.

The man who started Future Hope was Tim Grandage.

I first met Tim in a stark, grey office at the HongkongBank's headquarters in Hong Kong in 1990. He was a short, stocky man in his early thirties. While running one of the bank's branches in Calcutta, he had met some street children and started a home for a few boys, and just before we met he had resigned from the bank in order to work with the children full-time. Bankers don't do silly, impulsive things like that and Tim's colleagues weren't sure whether he was a saint or completely mad, but my first impression was of how sensible and solid he seemed. There was nothing of the crusader or religious zealot about him — he simply felt there was a job that had to be done.

'I won't spend the rest of my life doing this,' he told me, 'but I just feel that for the next few years I need to be there, to get things started.'

We discussed the nuts and bolts of organizing a charity — constitutions, committees, fund raising and publicity. I don't suppose I said anything particularly helpful, but as I was leaving Tim said, 'Come and see us, come and meet the kids.'

And so, seven years later, I did, going in search not of an individual but of an agency, knowing where to find it but not knowing quite what to expect.

Meeting the Children

Tim stopped his old green jeep and leaned out of the window to talk to a group of Future Hope boys coming home from school.

'Exam today?' he asked.

'Yes, uncle,' said one of the older boys. 'Geometry.'

'How was it?'

'Good.'

Tim laughed. 'Your mouth says good but your face says bad.'

The boy smiled. 'Well, not so good,' he admitted. 'But I passed.'

Coming home from school with their shirts hanging out of their trousers on a hot afternoon, the boys looked like any other middle-class children and it was easy to forget the horrors that each had endured. They smiled and chatted happily now, but in blacker times they had visited the farthest reaches of rejection and loneliness, had been dragged into realms of un-imaginable suffering.

One boy had been almost murdered by his father, who beat him terribly, cut his face and tried to throw him into a river. Another boy had been kept in a cupboard for two years because the family who employed his mother as a domestic servant refused to allow him to be seen in the house. He had been allowed out once at lunchtime and once in the evening.

'His skin was absolutely pale,' said Tim. 'He didn't laugh, he didn't play, he slept an incredible amount of the time — and then five months later he became hyperactive.'

'And now?'

'He's fine, a very loving child.'

Many children had run away to escape constant beatings by their fathers. Some were orphans and some had been thrown onto the streets after their fathers died and their mothers mar-ried men who wouldn't accept another man's children. And, in the vastness of India, some had literally lost their families.

'Probably the worst one was a boy we found on Sealdah Station,' said Tim. 'He'd been incredibly badly raped and had second degree syphilis.'

'How old was he?'

'Six or seven. He couldn't walk properly. His backside was completely ripped to pieces and we had to sit him in potassium permanganate for six months.'

I grimaced.

'It happens,' said Tim. 'A man feels randy on the station one night and he just takes the first person he can find.'

'But what about the emotional scars on the children?'

'What's very interesting is that many of them actually don't seem to be too badly affected. They don't seem to think it's a problem — it's just what adults do. They adapt to a different value system.'

'Are many of the children sexually abused on the station?'

'Well, it's only my figure but I would say about eighty per cent of them. It usually happens to the newer ones who have just arrived from the villages and are on their own.'

Most of Future Hope's children had been found on Calcutta's two major stations, Sealdah and Howrah, and it was still to the stations that Tim and his team went searching each week, looking for children who were alone and especially vulnerable.

'You will see children down there who are enjoying life, they're in a group of other children, they're not really in danger, ' said Tim, 'but we're looking for the ones who are running around on their own, the ones who are most vulnerable, who are desperate to come off.'

Boys such as Nizam.

Nizam

Nizam had been at Future Hope for six years and was one of the older boys, not sure of his exact age but 'sixteen plus'. He was small and neat, precise and serious. In a group of tumbling, teasing teenagers, Nizam had an unusual calmness and maturity. He was in Class 8 at one of Calcutta's best schools and doing well. University beckoned.

Yet six years earlier Nizam had been sleeping rough on the platforms of Sealdah Railway Station, alone and hungry, a ten-year-old boy a very long way from home.

Although he lacked formal education, Nizam had often helped his father in their small family shop and a tradesman's savvy helped him to survive in the big city.

As he watched sacks of fruit and vegetables being unloaded from trucks he noticed that some of the sacks split open and a few onions or potatoes fell to the ground, so he picked them up and sold them, making as much as twenty *rupees* on a good day, enough to feed himself. Bigger boys who were trying to make money in the same way resented him stealing their market and beat him up. He survived, but only just.

'I got really bad,' he said. 'Not enough to eat, clothes all torn, very dirty, sick. In the street you don't have a bath. I got lice — well, lice you can manage, but scabies is really no good and I got that too.'

The attack of scabies was serious and Nizam took himself off to the Brothers of Charity, who ran a Sunday drop-in centre for street children. He was so ill that the

Brothers kept him in for three months while he was being treated, although Nizam admitted to me with a smile that his scabies cleared up after a couple of weeks and that he stayed on only because he liked the comfort and the fact that he didn't have to fight for his food.

One day Tim visited the centre and agreed that Nizam could go to Future Hope the following week. A week passed but Tim didn't return, so Nizam, getting bored with comfort, devised a plan. He told a woman volunteer who was helping the Brothers that he would wait for one more week and that if Tim didn't return and take him to Future Hope within seven days he would take himself back to the station.

He smiled with pride as he got to the punchline of his story.

'When Tim uncle came again, this lady said to him, "You must take this boy because if you don't he's going to run away," and so Tim uncle took me home with him.'

'Do you really think you would have gone back to the station?' I asked.

'Of course!'

Nizam emphasised how lucky he was to be at Future Hope and to have had the chance to turn his life around, but he also wanted me to understand the value of having lived life in the raw. He had recently read a poem comparing the experiences of street children with those of children from middle-class apartments, and appreciated the poet's observation that, while street children live and eat and sleep with dogs, apartment children think dogs are toys made of wool.

'What do you think your time on the streets

taught you?' I asked.

He looked at me steadily. 'That I will survive,' he said. 'I will not die easily.'

'Do you regret any of the things you did back then, like stealing?'

'No. That was the situation at the time. If I didn't take advantage of it, I would have died. When you don't have a choice you must steal because, you know, we are all very selfish — we always want to live, we don't want to die.'

'Was there a lot of crime on the station?'

'Oh, yes. Murder, mugging, rape and... well, many things. I could lie to you but I won't. On the station, everything happens. Everything.'

I sensed there were memories he didn't want to stir.

'Do you still think about that time?' I asked.

'No,' he said. 'It's buried deep in my mind. Gone.'

Instead, Nizam was thinking about money — not for himself but to help his family. 'I have a twelve- or  thirteen-year-old brother,' he said, 'and the same thing is happening to him. He is not going to school. He has no education. Well, he may have a little of maths because of business — you know, learning to count, one, two, three — but that's all.' Nizam was praying for time to pass so that he could start earning money and give his brother the same sort of chance that he had enjoyed.

He wanted to be a businessman, but his attitude towards money was level headed and he hated to hear rich boys at school talking about it all the time. He told me of his experience with one particular boy.

'I said to him, "I like you, you're a nice kid, you're my best friend, but stop all this talk about money. My name is Nizam and money will never buy me. I will not become a servant of money. Money will be my servant." After that, he stopped. Then the other day I had a spare ticket for a concert and he wanted one for his mum and dad so I said to him, "Here, you can have this one." He said, "How much do you want for it?" and again I said to him, "I've told you, don't talk to me about money." The next day he bought me a drink, a Coca-Cola, and that was alright, but at least I didn't take money from a friend.'

After we had been talking for a couple of hours, I mentioned that in a discussion in one of the homes a few nights earlier a boy had asked me bluntly, 'Uncle, have you made any progress in your life?' The question, so stark and direct, had caught me by surprise and I had found myself struggling to justify forty-four years of little achievement.

Nizam listened and then said, without a hint of arrogance, 'Well, I can say I have done much progress in my life. Now I am educated. I can distinguish between the good and the bad. My parents were foolish. You know, if you just look at one side of your finger...'

He paused and smiled, looking down at my large white hands.

'Well, not your finger because yours is a different colour! But mine. You see, one side is dark and the other side is light, and my parents would look at one side and say, ah, you see this mark here. But now I say, wait, look at the other side. You have to look at the whole finger.'

Future Hope ran four homes in the south of Calcutta. Two were in one house, with the older boys downstairs and the

younger ones upstairs. Another was in a flat in a busy shopping area and the fourth was in the garden house of a mansion. All the premises were borrowed and eviction notices could be served at any time.

Wandering into one home on a sultry afternoon, I found a boy learning to touch type on an old computer, another on his knees washing clothes, five boys outside playing table tennis, another having his hair cut, Nizam scrubbing the floor, three of the younger boys peeling potatoes, one of the older ones out delivering a message, a boy called Shafique giving a magic show, some of the older lads lying on their beds revising for exams, two more playing chess and a group of the youngest ones making a vase of brightly coloured paper flowers as a farewell present for their teacher. A hive of activity.

Academic tuition was organized every evening after school but Saturday mornings were set aside for music and dance and it was wonderful to see the children's delight in their culture. I listened to Nizam, sitting on the floor beneath an open window, singing the songs of Rabindranath Tagore, eyes closed, lost in meanings and melodies. Manoj, who the previous evening had charged across a muddy rugby field to score a crucial try, was sitting in front of his tabla master, learning complex

rhythms. And one of the younger ones, Srinu, last seen thumping another boy during a fight on the bus home from football, was now dancing like a dream — sensuous, graceful, poised and incredibly expressive.

'That's the wonderful thing about Bengal,' said Tim.

'There is this huge love of music, of dance, of art. I don't know whether it's because they've been starved of it on the streets or because it's in their blood but our children love it. If you took a group of sixteen-year-olds in the UK and tried to make them do country dancing or sing folk songs they'd laugh you out of the place, but our children absolutely love it.'

Physical activities were a major feature of life at Future Hope. Countless boys told me about the time they all went trekking in Nepal, the adventure of a lifetime, and sport was part of the daily routine, with all the children coming together every afternoon to play football, rugby or cricket on fields in the centre of Calcutta racecourse. Sport improved the physical devel-

opment of children stunted by disease and malnutrition and taught all of them how to win and lose, how to follow rules, how to work in a team.

'I hope the thing about Future Hope is that whatever you are good at, whatever talents you have are brought out,' said Tim. 'Some hate rugby but love hockey, some prefer music and dance. Two or three years ago we did feel that we were too sports orientated and so we began to develop the arts — and won the Calcutta drama competition with a play which the children wrote themselves!'

Dheeraj

Dheeraj stopped me on the stairs.

'Hey, I've got a question for you,' he said. 'One word — "wanna". What means?'

I explained the contraction of want and to.

'OK,' he said. 'Gonna?'

I explained gonna, and then gotta and kinda.

'But they're not good English,' I said primly, 'they're

---

slang. Where did you hear them?'

He beamed at me. 'The Spice Girls!' he said.

Dheeraj was a classmate of Nizam at one of Calcutta's best schools but the two boys' characters were chalk and cheese. Dheeraj was the most garrulous of the older boys, words tumbling out of him. Many ideas were abandoned in mid-sentence as newer, more intriguing thoughts suddenly entered his mind. He was fluent in five languages — Assamese, Bengali, English, Hindi and Nepali — and spoke quickly and with tremendous passion. For Dheeraj, nothing was simply big, it had to be HUGE!

Even as a young boy in the northeastern state of Assam, Dheeraj had, by his own admission, been a bit of a handful.

'Yeah, I used to run away a lot. I didn't go to school. I used to go to watch TV. I was more interested in movies. This and that, you know. I didn't go home at night. Used to visit lots of places on the buses and trains. Yeah, my father used to beat me. Every time I got beaten, beaten, beaten, and so I made up my mind, you know, and said, "I'll really run away."'

He found a job for three months on a farm and then met up with some other children and together they made their way to Calcutta and on to Delhi. Dheeraj found a job in an hotel but left after a few weeks and lived rough on the streets. He was eleven years old.

I said, 'I can't imagine what that must be like. How did you survive?'

'In Delhi, it's not difficult. Any time you want food in

Delhi, food is there. I didn't worry about the food.'

'Did you beg?'

A momentary hesitation.

'Well, I wouldn't take twenty *paise* but if someone was giving ten *rupees* or twenty *rupees*, yeah, why not?'

Dheeraj was rescued from a street in Delhi when Tim went to visit veteran BBC correspondent Mark Tully and found Dheeraj and his friends asleep in the central reservation of a nearby road. The boys returned to Calcutta with Tim and, after a long train journey across India, arrived at Future Hope, shy and uncertain.

'I saw a lot of boys talking to Tim uncle,' he said. 'You know, they were all saying "Welcome back, uncle," all like that. Someone had drawn him a crocodile and I loved that painting. Still it comes in my mind. So then I started to do paintings and different things.'

Dheeraj had become a talented artist. He liked to paint on his own, when the other boys were sleeping, preferably in a room where the light was not too bright. He said he did his best work when he was feeling sad. He had recently changed his approach, and instead of painting cheerful traditional village landscapes or views of Howrah Bridge was using a more abstract style, much more complex and sombre. I couldn't comprehend the ideas behind the pictures, but perhaps for Dheeraj that was part of the attraction — he had found a style that allowed him to paint out his demons without revealing to the world his darkest secrets and private sadnesses.

When he ran away at the age of ten, his family heard nothing from him for almost four years. He couldn't write to them because he had forgotten his own address, but eventually he and Tim made the thirty-six hour train journey back to the tea gardens of Assam, to find his family.

'My heart was going da-ding, da-ding, da-ding and I was really shaking. You know, you're visiting your mum and dad. I got out of the car and everything looked the same, except some trees had come down. I know all the people, but nobody is recognizing me. You know, I say "Hello" but they're blind, they're not recognizing me. Funny thing is, my mother and father and brothers and cousins were all talking about me at that time and I was standing there in the door. Someone said "Sanu?" — that's my nickname — and then the crying and all that started.'

Since that visit Dheeraj had travelled home three times. His parents had told him not to worry about them and to concentrate on his studies.

'So do you ever think about Assam now?'

'Yeah, sometimes, when I hear slow music. On rainy days I remember Assam, because we have huge rains there, huge, much bigger than Calcutta.'

'And when you think of Assam what do you see?'

'I think about the mountains, the hills, the tea gardens, the cold air.'

'Do you think eventually you will go back there to work?'

'No.'

'Have you thought at all about what job you want to do?'

'I am not going to go into business,' he said with characteristic certainty. 'I am good at talking.' Short pause, big smile. 'Maybe I'll be a doctor.'

Many street children don't know how old they are or when their birthdays are, and new arrivals at Future Hope were often medically examined to determine their approximate age. Some were so traumatized that they didn't even know their own names. The younger they were, the easier it was to help them, but even a streetwise teenager would be given a home if he really wanted to make a new start.

'We've never really said we're full,' said Tim. 'We just squash up a bit more.'

Tim's wife, Erica, a nurse, looked after the children's health, supported by a network of friendly doctors. In the few days I was there she had to contend with a boy who contracted malaria, another who had stomach cramps and an older boy who needed to see a specialist after injuring his shoulder playing rugby. She was also trying to persuade one of the homes to give the boys less rice and a thicker, more nutritious *dhal*, although having watched the eleven boys wolf down a bucket of steaming rice at one sitting I reckoned they would take some convincing.

In the early days, when the children slept on the floor of Tim's flat, all were boys. A few girls had since been accepted but there were many more boys than girls on the streets. Tim reckoned one reason for this was that girls seemed to be more  tolerant of domestic violence and didn't run away so readily.

'Do you find that the girls have different problems and need different treatment?'

'No,' he said. 'A girl wants to be loved, wants to feel secure. Children on the streets have no worry about money, no worry about food, but the one thing they do lack is the security of a home.'

Many children told me that Future Hope had become like a family for them. Srinu, the fighting, dancing twelve-year-old, said, 'I feel Tim uncle is my daddy and Sophie [Tim's baby daughter] is my sister.' Three of the older boys told me that of all the many blessings they had received at Future Hope, the most valuable was love, a response which delighted Tim. 'It's not the material things,' he said, 'it's the values they get which are important.'

Future Hope did not promote one particular religious belief. Some children were Hindu, some were Muslim, some were Christian, and the different beliefs and customs of the various faiths were all respected.

Values were taught through countless small, everyday incidents and exercises which, step by step, helped the children to form — or reform — their ideas of right and wrong. This teaching depended, of course, on the Indian staff who ran the homes, who were on hand morning, noon and night to advise and encourage, to comfort and chastise.

One of them was Bikas Chatterjee, house parent of the small boys' home. He had joined Future Hope with no experience of childcare work, yet as we sat and chatted late into the evening he told me that he had found his life's vocation. He had twenty-six small boys in his care and not one of them was without problems, but Bikas treasured the opportunity to be able to help them grow.

The boys treated him like an older brother. 'Bikas-*da*, Bikas-*da*,' they called, and he broke off from whatever he was doing to resolve an argument, admire a new painting, help with homework, provide first aid, mend a broken toy, answer a question or simply listen. He rarely slept through the night, rising every couple of hours to administer medicines, to soothe away the horrors of a nightmare or to welcome a new boy who had just been rescued from the station. It was an arduous routine, one which left him with little or no time for himself, and yet I have never met a man who was happier in his work.

None of the Future Hope staff received big salaries — indeed, Tim and Erica received nothing at all — and there was no overtime pay for ridiculously long hours. The reward lay in the satisfaction of bringing children off the streets and helping them to grow into healthy, well-adjusted young adults.

'We are extremely lucky with the staff we have,' said Tim, 'extremely lucky. The trouble is that people like them are hard to find. If we are to grow, it's not the funding which will hold us back, it's not the premises, it's not the children — it's finding dedicated staff.'

Seeing the security and the love which surrounded the children and knowing how full their days were, it seemed almost inconceivable that any of them would want to leave, but surrendering the freedom of the streets was hard and most boys ran away at least once. The record holder, now a respected and settled senior boy, had bolted nineteen times.

'Something snaps inside,' said Tim. 'It's normally a situation when they haven't been able to face a problem. One of the major things we teach them is to face their problems. If you run to the station, you'll just get more problems.'

Even if a child did run away, the door to Future Hope was never closed. There would always be a shelter from the storm. 'We can never say to a child "Go out, and you can't come back" because you would never say that to your own son or daughter.'

Future Hope was licensed by the Department of Social Welfare, which monitored all agencies working with children, and the police had to be informed every time a child was taken in. These two measures reduced the risk of families being split up inadvertently, but the most effective safeguard was the fact that Future Hope tried to reunite every child with his or her family. Few of the youngsters said much about their families in the first few weeks, but as they settled down and began to trust the security of their new home they usually opened up and re-called their earlier lives. Once there was some firm information, Future Hope staff went with the child to try to find their miss-ing family.

'Everyone always says never take a child back to the fam-ily because they'll ask for money or cause you problems, but we've never found that,' said Tim. 'We try to reunite every pos-sible family, and there are only about twenty which we've been unable to contact. It's great fun, a bit like your search for the

book. We've been all over India on a train. You can't really plan these trips — you just have a general idea of where you're head-ing and then you jump trains as you go.'

When families were found, they al-most always asked Future Hope to con-tinue to care for their children, but Tim and his team encouraged the children to keep in touch and to pay regular visits home.

'Most of these reunions are wonderful to see, but they're very emotional. Mother and father are in floods of tears and there's a lot of wailing and shouting. Many of the children have run away because they did something wrong at home, and the parents have often been feeling incredibly guilty, and so the sense of relief on both sides is tremendous.'

However, in a few sad cases reunions were impossible.

Srinu

Take Srinu. (Well, actually his name at Future Hope was Sinu but he insisted to me that he wanted an 'r' between the 's' and the 'i', so there it is.) Srinu was twelve years old, small for his age, and, when he wasn't dancing, played scrum-half in the under-13s rugby team. His voice  was soft and husky and he had piercing hazel grey eyes. He was like a terrier, the type of boy for whom fight and fun were never more than a word apart.

In 1992, Srinu was rescued from Howrah Railway Station in a terrible state, speaking only Telagu, the language of Andhra Pradesh in south-eastern India. Gradually, his physical condition improved and by the time I met him he was fluent in both Hindi and English, but he still couldn't provide enough information on his background to enable a search to be made for his family. He thought he came from 'somewhere near Hyderabad.'

But one afternoon, sitting cross-legged on a bed, Srinu told me he was sure that his mummy knew where he was.

'How does she know?' I asked.

'See, uncle,' he said, holding his hands in front of him with his thumbnails next to each other. 'She puts oils on here. Then she goes into the sunshine and then she can see me.'

It seemed the most natural thing in the world. Didn't every boy's mother do the same?

'You know, uncle, why she is not coming here to Future Hope? Because if she come here she cannot speak Bengali and the police would beat her. Otherwise, she would come and see me.'

'Do you think about your mummy a lot?'

'Yes. I dream about my mummy and my father and my sisters. You know, uncle, I dreamed I found them! Then, I waked up and —' he shut his eyes tightly for a moment and then blinked them wide open '— see nobody. I cried so much, so much.'

'Remember the first time we met?' I said to Tim. 'You said you wouldn't be working with street children for the rest of your life, that you just wanted to get something started.'

He laughed. 'And now we are tied in, totally and completely, which is extremely daunting, sometimes extremely frightening. I hope, of course, that we can train up an Indian person who can do a better job and take over, but I accept that for the rest of my life, for the rest of Erica's life, we will be involved with these children.'

'But,' I suggested, 'a critic might say that what you are doing is no more than a drop in the ocean, helping a hundred children in a city where hundreds of thousands are destitute.'

'Absolutely true. It *is* just a drop in the ocean. The only way you're going to solve the problems of millions of children on the streets is not to work at the curative end, taking them off the streets, but to change the attitudes of people at the top of the society — and the only way you'll do that is to convince them that children on the streets are at least as good as, if not better than, other children.'

That was why the sporting triumphs of Future Hope boys

were so important. People hearing that 'the street boys' had just walked away with Calcutta's under-13, under-16 and under-19 rugby championships might reconsider their prejudices. Future Hope depended entirely on donations and the fact that more and more funds were being raised in Calcutta suggested that the city's residents were becoming more concerned about the tragedy in their midst.

'But,' I persisted, 'when you see so many children on the streets and in the stations, don't you sometimes think the situation is hopeless?'

'No, I don't think it's hopeless,' said Tim, 'and I don't know why I don't think it's hopeless! Perhaps I am naive enough to think that you can have a go at anything. In the end it will boil down to education. If you can educate a very large population in health care and population control, then you have a chance.'

In the meantime, Future Hope was giving at least some children an opportunity to break free.

'Some boys have gone back to the streets,' said Tim. 'I bumped into one at five-thirty this morning on Howrah Station. Only one, I think, was a total failure, a boy who is now a drug addict with a wife and a child. We got him quite late and he was much less educated than the others. He didn't think much about what he was doing, he was more driven by physical needs. He still rings up about once a week and when his baby was born he came to show us on the fourth day, so I suppose it's not a total failure, but we wanted better for him.'

'How do you measure success?' I asked.

'Success is a person who is happy, who is well settled and who can look after themselves to a standard that they're comfortable with, certainly better than on the street, and who can give something back to society. A lot of our boys are now getting good jobs — not high-flying jobs but good jobs — and if you can reintegrate them into society, that's where success is, because a street child is outside society.'

There was one other point which intrigued me about Future Hope. I had seen many agencies working with street children in many countries, most run by professional social workers. Yet Future Hope, the agency which had impressed me more than any other, was run by — in the best sense of the word — amateurs. Tim had been a bank manager, Bikas a security guard.

'We feel very strongly that children want and need ordinary people,' said Tim. 'The people who tend to get most information from the children about their backgrounds are the cooks, when they're helping to peel potatoes or make *chapattis*. Children don't need sophisticated, educated people who counsel them — they need people who really care about them and, most important, who have a lot of time for them. Children need time.'

That said, there were certain things which were fundamental to Future Hope's work. The first was that you had to provide a real home for the children because that was what they most lacked. The home should not promote any particular religious belief or political agenda but should be a place where every talent could blossom. It must go beyond the basics of food, shelter, clothing and education and help children to develop their own morality.

'The stress more and more and more has to be on values,' said Tim. 'Some of the unhappiest people in the world have everything and give nothing, and several of the happiest people I know have nothing but give everything.'

Konda

Just across the road from Queen's Mansions on busy Park Street was the Oxford bookstore and gallery, a cool oasis of calm, a place designed to encourage browsing. Konda, a Future Hope graduate, worked there.

'I joined the bookshop in August this year,' he told me, 'and I am doing everything. Salesman's work, the computer, filing the papers — many things I have to learn about the books and how to attend to all the customers.'

A bookshop seemed the ideal environment for Konda, who was much quieter and more serious than most of the youngsters at Future Hope, slightly shy, meticulous, polite and considerate. Had I not heard his life story I might almost have dismissed him as mild and ineffectual, but in truth he was a man as tough as tungsten.

He was living in a rented room with two other Future Hope graduates, one working for an airline and the other an electrical repairman. Tim had been paying their rent to help them get started but they were about to take over and become completely independent.

'Why do you still go back to Future Hope every week?' I asked Konda.

'Because I have to give Tim uncle the respect that he has given me a new life,' he said. 'We lose our father and mother but now Tim uncle is our father and mother, our everything.'

'But I'm sure Tim doesn't want you to come back every week just because of him.'

Konda smiled and tilted his head.

'But I feel like this,' he said quietly.

Konda was born in the state of Orissa in eastern central India to a blind father and a sick mother. He had one
younger brother. His parents fought often and
Konda remembered his father tying him to a
bed and beating him. After a few years, his
parents separated and Konda went off with his
mother. One day, sitting with her on a railway
station somewhere in Bihar, Konda felt thirsty
and went to get a drink. When he returned his
mother had vanished. He was seven or eight
years old and suddenly utterly alone.

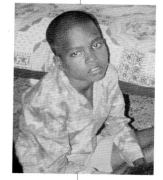

His seemed to have been a childhood of such unre-
mitting sadness and dislocation that I wondered whether
he recalled any good times.

'What was the happiest moment of your childhood?' I asked.

He thought for a while and then smiled gently. 'I
never got the happiest moment,' he said.

For five years, one extraordinary little boy travelled
the length and breadth of eastern India, looking for his
mother. He worked for a time on a farm and at one stage
was taken in by a Muslim family, but the aching need to
find his mother drove him on. Eventually, he ended up
on the platform of Calcutta's Howrah Station, where Tim
found him and gave him a home. He made a late start on
his education, went on to technical college and eventually landed his job at the renowned Oxford bookstore.
His progress in eight years had been extraordinary.

One day he and Tim went back to Bihar and Orissa,
to see if they could find his parents, but the trip ended in
sadness. Relatives told him that his father had died and

they believed that his mother was also dead. He could hope no longer and knew that he was alone.

'I remember the moment he heard the news,' said Tim. 'His expression didn't change one bit.' It wasn't that Konda was past caring, but he had somehow developed an extraordinary capacity to absorb sadness and disappointment, telling himself always that he must, in his favourite phrase, 'stand on my feet.'

'I am happy with my new life,' he said. 'I worry about my mother and father, that I lose them, but it's a remembered thing, not a living thing. Tim uncle has given me a new life.'

Although Konda did not find his parents, he did rediscover his younger brother and, with Tim's encouragement, brought him to Future Hope. This was his proudest achievement, to see Munsing settled in the small boys' home.

'I cannot see my father, but I feel that if he can see us he will be glad with us,' he said.

Konda was saving most of the money he earned for the day when he would marry and start a family. Creating a loving home for his own children would be his greatest satisfaction.

'I want to make them every time happy,' he said. 'I will give them good education. I will work hard for them. I will never beat them — I never used to beat anybody. I will tell them, make them understand.'

I asked Konda what he did when children approached him on the street and begged for money. After all, he was now a working man with some money in his pocket. He said he didn't give money because it might be

wasted on alcohol or drugs, but he some-
times gave food. Then he mentioned, almost
as an afterthought, that one boy on Park
Street had recently asked for his help in getting a job and, through a former classmate
who worked for a telephone paging com-
pany, he had been able to do it. In fact, he joked, the boy
was earning almost as much as he was.

Later, I recounted this story to Tim.

'I hadn't heard that,' he said, 'but it's typical Konda.
Where on earth he gets his values from after the life he's
had I just don't know, but he's spot on every time.'

A Smudge on the Platform

Half past midnight, Howrah Station.

We parked the jeep behind some trucks and walked towards the station's main entrance. I was quietly apprehensive
about what I might see and how I would react, but for Tim this
was just a routine visit, checking for children in danger. He was
not hunting for a particular boy or girl, not expecting to pluck a
child from the platform this night. He just wanted to show his
face and keep in touch.

'Because we go frequently, other children will refer me to
kids in trouble,' he said.

On the road outside the station a man and four filthy, di-
shevelled children were sleeping huddled together under a
street lamp. I thought they looked in a terrible state but Tim
was unconcerned.

137

'You always like to see women and children sleeping in a place where there's some light,' he said, 'because it makes it more difficult for people to interfere with them.'

Inside the vast station hall, the daily tide of passengers had ebbed. A few hours earlier the platforms had been seething with people making their various ways into and out of the city, but at this late hour there was little movement. People were settling down for the night — hundreds upon hundreds of them, bedding themselves down on rush mats, sheets of newspaper, the bare platform.

We walked down one platform, passing a group of about fifty homeless people watching a late night movie on the station's television monitor.

'I really think that's one reason why so many street children are so small and poorly developed,' said Tim. 'They don't sleep properly, just short bursts of two or three hours at a time.'

As we moved further down, the number of sleepers decreased. There was more space between the bodies. Single men, a few old people, two mothers huddled together with five young children. Behind one pillar was a middle-aged man, dressed only in a red *lungi*, having his leg massaged by a young boy.

'That's how they get into prostitution,' said Tim quietly as we passed.

We were nearing the end and Tim suggested we jump down onto the tracks and cross to the next platform, but just at that moment we spotted a body some way ahead, a small dark smudge.

'Here's a little one,' said Tim. 'Let's have a look.'

The little one was a boy, six or perhaps seven years old, filthy dirty and dressed only in a pair of black shorts. He was sound asleep on the platform and had taken off his vest to use as a pillow.

Tim bent down and tried to wake him.

'Come on, little one,' he said in Bengali. 'Wake up. What's your name?'

At first, the boy didn't stir. He was in a deep sleep. Then, as Tim continued to talk to him, he lashed out with his arms as though trying to protect himself, and  shouted a few words in Hindi. This, said Tim, was the reaction not of a boy used to being woken by his mother but of one who expected to be abused.

'We should try to get him in,' he said.

The boy sat up, rubbed his eyes and began to scratch himself.

'He doesn't speak Bengali so I'll go and find a couple of other lads who can speak to him in Hindi,' said Tim. 'You stay here with him.'

I looked around. The station was dim and cavernous and we were sitting a long way down the platform, under a sign saying Coach 14. This little lad was the very last body and beyond us the rail tracks snaked away into the night. A late train rolled slowly into a distant platform and squeaked to a halt. Down between the rails, a man was defecating. There was an eerie stillness to the place, like being in the eye of a typhoon.

I tried to talk to the boy but drew no response. He just kept his eyes closed and continued to scratch himself. After a  time he gave a little sigh, lay down on the platform and went back to sleep. I looked at my watch. It was one o'clock.

Tim returned with a couple of boys in their late teens or early twenties and they woke the little one again and spoke to him in Hindi. He told them that his name was Santosh but any more information was either too difficult or too painful for him to recall. One of the boys, Bapi, suggested to Santosh that he should go with us, assuring him that Tim would take good care of him. The little boy seemed to consider this for a moment and then stood up, picked up his vest from the platform and put it on. He took hold of Bapi's hand and we began to walk slowly back up the platform.

I remarked to Tim on how helpful Bapi was being.

'It's quite humbling, isn't it?' he said. 'Children on the streets can be incredibly gentle and incredibly kind in a very harsh environment. These two may be doing all sorts of rackets in the daytime and they don't want to come off the streets themselves, but they'll still help another kid.'

As we emerged from the station concourse, taxi drivers crowded around us in search of business, but we made our way steadily back to the jeep and sat Santosh between us. Tim started the engine and as we began to move forward Bapi stuck his head through the open window and said to the little lad, 'You stay well. You're going to a place with a big heart. Don't run away.'

We rattled across the station forecourt and over Howrah Bridge, Santosh pulling himself forward to peer over the dashboard as we raced through the night. He still seemed half asleep and I wondered whether in the morning he would remember any of this.

'He will remember this night much longer than you will,' said Tim.

We sped on across the Maidan and along deserted streets.

'What will the other boys say when they wake up tomorrow morning and find there's a new boy among them?' I asked Tim.

'Oh, I don't know — "Silly old uncle's been down to the station again," I should think.'

Eight minutes after leaving the station we arrived at Future Hope's home for small boys. The security guard let us in and we climbed the stairs in darkness, Santosh holding Tim's hand, and then at the entrance of the main bedroom Tim switched on the light. Two rows of small boys were spread across the floor, all sound asleep, arms and legs splayed in every direction, exhausted by the day's activities, dreaming of their heroic feats on the football field. Above all, safe.

Santosh looked on, silent and wide-eyed.

Tim was due at the airport to meet a colleague arriving on a late flight, so he roused the house parent, Bikas, introduced him to Santosh and left.

Bikas went to the store room, chose a clean set of clothes from the 'Small' pile and then led Santosh into the bathroom. The little boy was, not surprisingly, bewildered but Bikas quietly explained what they were going to do, his voice comforting, encouraging, beginning to teach. Santosh took off his vest and shorts and Bikas began pouring water over his head, talking to him gently as he opened a new bar of soap and began to scrub. The suds were black. Bikas took care cleaning Santosh's knee, where there was a wound which the boy said had been caused by falling off a train. He washed him again and this time

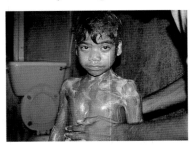

the suds were merely grey. The third time, brown.

I squatted down beside Santosh and took some photos. To start with, he looked at me blankly but suddenly the flashlight sprang open and his

surprised face broke into a broad grin. It was a magical moment, like watching a butterfly emerge from a chrysalis.

Bikas wrapped Santosh in a towel and helped him into his new clothes — a pair of grey shorts and a white T-shirt. All the time he was talking to him in Hindi, telling him where to put his dirty clothes, explaining toilet drill.

'And after you go to the toilet you come and wash your hands here,' he said, turning on a tap at the washbasin. Santosh was amazed to see how the tap worked and spent a couple of minutes turning it on and off, laughing as the water alternately gushed and stopped. Bikas combed Santosh's hair with his fingers and, as we left the bathroom, the little boy jumped up to switch off the light.

Bikas laid out a bed roll on the floor and Santosh lay down. Bikas pulled a sheet over him and whispered that he would be sleeping just next door. Santosh closed his eyes and was out like a light.

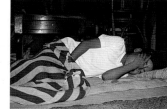

I looked at my watch. Two o'clock. Exactly one hour earlier I had been sitting with him on that grim, ghostly platform at Howrah Station. In one hour, a little boy had found hope for the future.

*   *   *

When he woke up the next morning, Santosh had a haircut and Tim's wife, Erica, gave him a quick physical check-up.

'The externals seem not too bad,' she said, 'but I'm not so sure about the internals.'

A distended belly suggested worms and Erica noted an unhealthy yellowness in his eyes. A full medical examination would follow and Santosh would be deloused and dewormed. Letters would be sent to the police and the Social Welfare Department, informing them that Santosh had been admitted, and, as details of his story emerged, efforts would be made to reunite him with his family.

Santosh recognized another boy, Romesh, who had been brought in from Howrah almost six weeks earlier. That suggested that he had been living on the station for some time, but all he would say on that first morning was that his mother had sent him off begging and that he didn't know where she was.

I challenged Tim about the previous evening's rescue. Suppose Santosh's mother had also been on the station and had just left him for a while, I said. She would now be distraught, searching high and low for her son.

'If his mother is with him in Calcutta, she certainly hadn't been in contact with him for some time,' he said. 'You could see he was very traumatized and the fact that he was sleeping so far down the platform shows that he was on his own. But if his mother is there we'll find her and reunite them.'

The other boys were extraordinarily helpful and welcoming, and Konda's brother, Munsing, a fluent Hindi speaker, was put in charge of showing Santosh around. Some children were very quiet and overawed when they were first admitted, while others were insecure and aggressive, but Santosh was just inquisitive, wanting to open every cupboard, try every toy, join every game.

'All day he is asking me questions!' said Bikas. 'Over the next few weeks he will have a thousand, thousand questions.'

In the late afternoon, all the children piled into the Future Hope bus and headed for the sports field. The younger ones, of whom Santosh was very much the youngest and shortest, were going to play football. Teams were chosen, Bikas blew his whistle and play began. Little Srinu took off his shirt and was soon in the thick of the action, tackling with characteristic determination, eyes never leaving the ball, but Santosh didn't have the first clue what was going on. He just ran wherever the other children ran and sometimes stopped to take Bikas's arm or to ask yet another question.

Then, just before the final whistle, a hazy cloud of dragonflies drifted low across the field, gossamer wings glinting in the golden light of a setting sun. Santosh caught sight of them and stopped in his tracks, gazing up in wonder. His face broke into a wide-eyed smile and, forgetting all about football, he started to run around on his own, clapping his hands with delight, jumping into the air and trying to catch dragonflies, a picture of innocence and happiness.

CHAPTER 6

India, West Bengal
Sibdaspur

Mrs. Sajahan

Counting Chickens

On March 23, 1988, Mrs. Sajahan and I spent half an hour trying to catch chickens.

We were in the village of Sibdaspur, about eighty kilometres north of Calcutta. An agency called the Centre for Social Development (CSD) was trying to alleviate poverty and raise health standards in poor communities, and Mrs. Sajahan was one of ten women who had been given a loan by CSD to start a small business. The programme, including the women's loans, was funded by Oxfam Hong Kong.

Mrs. Sajahan, a tall, thin woman with protruding teeth, had received 100 *rupees* and had used the money to buy four chicks. By the time I and a couple of CSD workers arrived in Sibdaspur a few months later, those four chicks had become thirty-one.

Mrs. Sajahan said the chicks would be a very useful source of extra income because she had three young children to feed

and her husband was a landless labourer whose income fluctuated with the seasons. She produced a card to prove that she
had been repaying her loan in regular instalments, and she had
acknowledged receipt of the original 100 *rupees* not with a sig-
nature but with a thumbprint.

We told her how pleased we were to see that things were
going well, that we wished we could stay longer but that we
had many projects to see that day and so had to be on our way.
We rose to leave — but Mrs. Sajahan wasn't having that. She insisted that we had to see each and every bird.

She walked across the patch of bare earth in front of her
hut, calling to the chicks and scattering a little feed in the dust.
A few chicks emerged, and she then walked over to some trees
and called again. A few more chicks came clucking out of the
undergrowth, and as each newcomer appeared Mrs. Sajahan
tried to count them. The trouble was that every time a few
chicks appeared on the left, those on the right headed back into
the bushes or disappeared behind the house.

After this game had gone on for fifteen minutes we told
Mrs. Sajahan that we could see she had a lot of chicks and were
happy to accept her assurance that the total number was indeed
thirty-one. Still she wouldn't give up, and we realized that the
only way we were ever going to get out of Sibdaspur was by becoming cowboys at the Sajahan corral. So I went one way, the CSD
workers went the other and, with much flailing of arms and flapping of wings, we began to drive the hapless chicks back towards
Mrs. Sajahan. Finally, she decided the whole flock had assembled
and made a quick count. All present and correct. Thirty-one.

And then, before I could even take a photo of them, the in-
fernal birds scattered in all directions!

Nine years on, I wanted to find Mrs. Sajahan and see how

her chicken business was going because it had seemed to have the potential not only for boosting her income but also for improving the health of her children and for empowering her, a woman in a poor Muslim community.

'If she's continued the way she started,' said a friend, 'she'll have a battery farm by now. Hope she doesn't want you to count them all this time.'

A Grand Occasion

We set off early from Calcutta, heading north towards the town of Barrackpore. The map showed a straight line called the Barrackpore Trunk Road, which sounded like a major highway but was, of course, the usual leisurely confusion of people and animals, overcrowded buses and broken down trucks. We bullied and braked our way through the crowds, horn blaring and clouds of black exhaust fumes puffing in through our open windows. A young social worker from one of CSD's urban centres in Calcutta, Anirban Mitra, was travelling with me, paying his first visit to Sibdaspur, and his crisply laundered white shirt became greyer and more crumpled the further we travelled through the fumes and heat.

After a couple of hours we skirted Barrackpore and were onto smaller roads, stopping occasionally to ask for directions. There was little traffic now — two men pushing a cart stacked high with enormous bamboo poles, a boy leading a goat, the occasional brightly painted truck.

Then we turned off onto an even narrower track and began to wind our way across the fields to Sibdaspur. Bright green rice fields stretched away on either side and we had to slow down to avoid sending cyclists tumbling into the paddy. The track was a children's playground, a place for drying rice, as good a place as any to stand and talk. It twisted past bamboo groves and stands of banana trees and crossed small streams. The air smelt fresher and the big black city faded from memory like a bad dream at dawn.

Sibdaspur was not so much a village as a scattering of huts and small farms. The physical centre of the community seemed

to be a junction of three tracks, with a small shop and a lot of men standing around chatting. Bicycles were propped against trees, handcart owners waited for loads and dogs stretched out in sleep. Even at mid-morning there was an air of lazy afternoon.

Now that I think back, I remember CSD's president Dr. Niyogi did say something about opening a new building before we went to meet Mrs. Sajahan, but I was totally unprepared for what awaited us in Sibdaspur. The *panchayat* or village council had given some land next to its own building and CSD had

built a long, single-storey, cream-coloured building which was to be a health and education centre, community hall, vocational training centre and area office. This was the day of the official opening and it was clearly going to be quite a ceremony.

The new community centre, close to the junction of the tracks but set back across a patch of grass, was by far the smartest building in Sibdaspur. It was decorated with rings of flowers and vases of orange marigolds, and a red ribbon was stretched across the entrance steps. Announcements boomed from a loudspeaker and women and children began to gather for the cel-

ebrations. At first, they stood some distance away in the shade
of trees, but as the hour approached and the
crowd swelled, they began to press towards
the building, a glorious riot of colour.

'One thing I forgot to mention,' said
the genial Dr. Niyogi. 'We hope you'll agree
to be a guest of honour.'

Hoots from large conch shells announced the start of the
ceremony and a local parliamentarian stepped forward to cut
the red ribbon. A firecracker exploded beside us and we proc-
essed into the building under a shower of marigold petals. The
crowd of villagers paid no heed to honoured guests and barged
past us, laughing and shouting, in an effort to secure the best
seats. This was their building and they had waited a long time
for this day. They were going to enjoy the next couple of hours.

We took our seats on the stage and were presented with
corsages of wilting rosebuds, and I looked at the audience
seated expectantly in front of us. There were more than three
hundred people packed into the hall, sitting so closely together
on the floor that a photographer could hardly find a spot between them to place his feet. There were people standing
around the walls and children peeping in at the windows, cling-
ing onto the bars and craning their necks to get a better view.

There wasn't a man amongst them. Plenty of men were
standing around in the centre of the village and as the ceremony continued a few who couldn't contain their curiosity
came and stood outside the hall, listening to what was happening inside, but this was very much an occasion for the women
of Sibdaspur. Ironically, apart from Dr. Niyogi's wife, all the
guests of honour were men.

A woman in the front row of the audience, wearing a

beautiful peach-coloured sari, beamed at me as if we were old friends. I smiled back but had no idea who she was, remembering Mrs. Sajahan as being much slimmer, yet every time our eyes met this woman inclined her head and smiled at me, not just with her mouth but with her eyes.

The ceremony went on for a long time. Fans whirred over the audience but the one over the stage had been removed to allow extra lighting to be installed and so we sat there for two hours drenched in sweat. I felt like an ice cube under a sunlamp.

Three young dancers took turns to entertain the audience, each of them exquisitely painted and dressed in brilliantly coloured saris and chains of silver and gold. There were many false starts as the wrong music was played and cassette tapes were frantically rewound or changed. At one point, in the middle of a dance, the sound system gave up completely but the dancer continued as though nothing had happened and nobody took their eyes off her; these were much loved old standards and the music was playing in people's heads.

A small harmonium was placed in the centre of the stage, the rusty microphone stands were adjusted and three singers sang Bengali songs. The audience swayed gently to the rhythm of the tabla.

There were the inevitable speeches and only Dr. Niyogi had the good sense to keep his remarks short. The parliamentarian went on for what seemed an eternity, haranguing his bored audience. The louder and more agitated he became, the more obviously the crowd ignored him, and, after a rousing conclusion which drew only derisory applause, he pleaded another engagement and left.

At the front of the stage was a stack of six circular brass trays, with wicks laid around the edges of each tray in tiny pools of oil. I was invited to light the first wick and to say a few words, which I duly did, saying what a pleasure it was to return to Sibdaspur on such an auspicious day and congratulating the community on their new building. Looking at the audience, I reckoned at least one third of them hadn't been born when I had last visited.

One by one the honoured guests made their excuses and left the stage until there was only Dr. and Mrs. Niyogi and myself left. They were still looking cool, calm and collected but I was drenched in sweat, beads of perspiration dripping from my eyebrows.

The ceremony ended and we left the stage, emerging into the glare of the afternoon sun which, after the heat inside, felt like an alpine breeze. We went into a side room and saw a display of CSD's work — handpainted sticks with which children were taught to count, bold and simple health education posters, attractive bags made from old trousers, a useful source of supplementary income for the women who sewed them.

Outside, on the grassy area in front of the building, the women of Sibdaspur stood in small groups chatting, and the moment I saw them I knew that this picture would remain in my mind's eye long after details of the ceremony had faded. There were saris in the most exotic shades of green and gold, blue and purple, pink and maroon, and the women's lustrous black hair glistened in the sunlight. Those rich, vibrant colours are scorched into my memory.

The women stood there for a long time, talking and laughing with each other. The show was over but nobody wanted to go home. Packing away their best saris would mean there was nothing more to look forward to.

'A highlight,' said Dr. Niyogi, 'if not of their whole lives, at least the highlight of this year.'

Signs of Progress

There were some 42,000 people scattered across the villages and farms around Sibdaspur, almost all of them Bengalis. Roughly half were Muslims and half Hindus but Dr. Niyogi said there was no animosity between the communities. They were well established and many families had been in the area for generations.

'I should say the people here are typical rural Bengali people,' said Dr. Niyogi, himself a native of Barrackpore.

People were poor. Most families had no land and the men worked as casual labourers. Family incomes were often as low as 600 or 800 *rupees* per month.*

'That's a very small amount of money,' said Dr. Niyogi. 'You only can just survive.'

What money there was was not always spent to good effect.

'Drinking is quite rampant in these areas,' he said. 'In most of the villages there's a drinking den.'

'That's a bit surprising, isn't it,' I said, 'with so many people being Muslims?'

'Well, they do drink quite a bit,' said Dr. Niyogi, 'even though it is a religious taboo. In fact, I can tell you that the Muslim people drink more than the Hindus!'

The Centre for Social Development (CSD) had originally

* US$1 = 40 *rupees*

focused on improving health standards and on my first visit
nine years earlier I had stumbled across a scene that looked like
a picture from a rural health manual.
Two young health workers had arrived on bicycles in the neighbouring village of Ramchandrapur and in
the comfortable shade of an old
mango tree were immunizing children against polio, diphtheria,

whooping cough and tetanus. Health education posters were
hanging from the branches of the tree with a few more hanging
on a bullock cart nearby. A crowd of children waited with mothers and fathers, brothers and sisters, and forty children were
vaccinated during the day, all free of charge.

Over the years, like so many agencies, CSD decided that
clinics and vaccination programmes were not enough. The reali-
zation that many health problems resulted from sheer poverty
led to projects to help women boost their family incomes; Mrs.
Sajahan was one of the first beneficiaries. These projects led on
to the formation of women's groups in many villages, which in
turn began to challenge traditional gender stereotypes. The
stark fact that many families had too little food for too many
mouths led to family planning programmes and efforts to in-
crease food production. Village *balwadis* or kindergartens were
started in a long-term effort to raise educational standards.

This integrated programme of social and economic development was now ten years old and so, as we sat on the shaded verandah of the *panchayat* building, I asked Dr. Niyogi whether he
had seen any changes in the community as a result of all this work.

'Oh, yes,' he said. 'Take awareness of family planning, for
example. The birth rate used to be forty per thousand per year,

but now it's down to between twenty-five and twenty-six per thousand. If we can continue our work, we'll be able to get it down below twenty, which is quite reasonable.

'There's much more self-awareness among the women. They used to be completely dependent on their menfolk. If the

men earned something, they could eat. If they didn't, they starved. Ten years ago, we used to have to sell the idea of income generation to the women, but now they come to us and tell us to organize something so that they can earn some money. That's a great change. You see this morning how women are coming forward for community events. Before they used to be behind the curtain. There is now, more or less, a bit of equilibrium. It used to be entirely male dominated but now, it's not completely balanced but women do have quite something to say. Five of the fifteen *panchayat* members here are women and the chairman is a Muslim woman.

'We see changes in education. With the introduction of *balwadis*, all families now try to send their boys to school, at least until they are ten or twelve and a few go on to secondary. Before, there was almost no education for girls but now we see that's changing.

'The other change, I think, is health consciousness. Before, if people were ill they would go to rural... well, I suppose you would call them quacks. They had no medicines at all. Nowadays they come to our health centres where there is a qualified medical person. People are very much conscious about immunizing children. We are not actually doing immunization ourselves now but we do tell them where to go for it. The government centres are now working quite well — they used to be quite idle but now they have to work!'

Not that Dr. Niyogi thought CSD's work in Sibdaspur was finished. Over the next ten years, he hoped to see family sizes reduced still further and every child completing at least primary education. There were plans to train people in inland fish farming, vegetable farming and beekeeping, and to help women form a handicraft cooperative. CSD's health centres, he said, would introduce a simple insurance scheme to allow families to receive free general medical services for a monthly fee of five *rupees*.

After outlining these hopes for the future, Dr. Niyogi took me across to the new community centre to meet a woman whose own story reflected the progress of the past. Her name was Rabeya Bibi and she was wearing a blouse of harsh green, wrapped in a sari of the most delicate colours — lavender, champagne and powder blue. We sat around a table in a barely furnished office and before I even had time to open my notebook the room filled with more than thirty other women and a few men who stood and listened to us. It was a slow conversation, for although Dr. Niyogi and Rabeya both spoke Bengali, he thought she might feel intimidated or shy if he questioned her directly and so every question was repeated by CSD worker Sikha Majumder, who knew Rabeya well and sat close beside her.

Like Mrs. Sajahan, Rabeya had been given a loan of 100 *rupees* and had used it to buy four chicks. The loan was repaid and the eggs sold. Rabeya took another loan and bought a calf. The calf grew into a cow and she was able to sell the milk. Then she went for the big time, borrowing 1,000 *rupees* and buying a motorized rickshaw which could transport vegetables from the village to the town. She opened her own bank account and rented out the rickshaw to her husband for ten *rupees* per day.

'Can you give me some examples of how your family's situation has changed as a result of your success?' I asked.

First and foremost, she said, she now had enough food to feed her family properly. She was able to buy better clothes for

herself and her children and to make sure that they had something new to wear at festival time. The family used to live in a rented hut but now they had a place of their own — it was only a mud hut but at least it was their own.

Rabeya had four cows, twelve hens and thirty or forty chicks, which between them earned her an average of 300 *rupees* per month. Her husband and children helped to look after the animals, carrying heavy things for her and helping when a cow needed to see a vet.

'My husband is quite helpful,' she said.

In addition to being helpful, Rabeya's husband had one of life's more unusual jobs, going into the mango orchards around the village and collecting ants' eggs, which he then sold to fish farmers as food for their young fish. The trouble was that the eggs were not available all year round and so he used to spend a few months of the year idle, but now that he was a rickshaw driver as well as an egg collector his income was much steadier. When he was busy collecting eggs, he sublet the rickshaw to someone else.

As for Rabeya — well, she had really got the bit between her teeth. Not content with her agricultural successes, she was learning tailoring and thinking of buying her own sewing machine, so that she could earn extra money by making clothes for a shop in Calcutta. She was also starting to educate herself. She had been absolutely illiterate but was learning to read and write through CSD's informal education programme. Her daughter was married and had recently given birth to her first grandson, but her two sons were still at school and she hoped they would continue up to matriculation. She was convinced that children these days were more intelligent than her own generation.

Rural India does not change quickly or easily, but Sibdaspur was clearly a developing community. Dr. Niyogi had been able to point to specific examples of progress over the past ten years and Rabeya was justifiably pleased with her achievements. I joked with her that she would surely win Sibdaspur's Businesswoman of the Year award.

But I hadn't come to Sibdaspur to open a community centre or to meet Rabeya. I had come to find Mrs. Sajahan and, though nothing had been said of her — or perhaps *because* nothing had been said of her — I was beginning to suspect that her story might not be so happy.

A Woman's Life

We walked along the main track heading out of the village and then turned off along a smaller stone path, shaded by trees. I was trying to get my bearings, looking for something to trigger my memory, but could find no clues, no recollection of having been there before.

We turned onto a dirt path and walked about twenty metres into a small clearing where four mud huts stood around a patch of bare ground. Some children spotted us first and then a tan and white dog, basking in the sun, raised its head and let

out a long howl of alarm. A woman emerged from one of the huts and I recognized her as the friendly face from the morning's celebrations. She had changed into a working sari but still wore her beaming smile.

'As soon as I saw him this morning I remembered him,' she said to one of CSD's workers. 'I remember him coming a long time ago and chasing the chickens.'

Then, out of another hut across the little compound, stepped another woman, dressed in a purple sari covered with brightly coloured designs. She was a rather gaunt figure with a crimson stud in the side of her nose, plain rings in her ears and two plastic bracelets on one wrist.

'Ah,' I said to Anirban, 'that's Mrs. Sajahan.'

'Well, nobody would ever call her that,' he said, explaining that Sajahan was her husband's name and that she was known by her own name of Mumtaz Begum, an elementary point which I had missed nine years earlier.

Anirban and I were ushered under the overhanging roof of one of the huts to escape the sun and invited to sit on a table covered with a brightly coloured cloth, surrounded by a gaggle of giggling, curious children. Mumtaz joined us and slowly we began to piece together the story of one woman in one small corner of India.

Mr. Sajahan was the eldest of four brothers and the four huts in the compound were for the four brothers' families. Eight adults and fifteen children lived there and the woman who had been so welcoming was one of Mumtaz's three sisters-in-law.

Mumtaz herself had been an orphan, born in a neighbouring village, and had married Mr. Sajahan at the age of seventeen. It was an arranged marriage — she had seen her husband once before but the first time they spoke to each other was on their wedding day. On my previous visit nine years earlier the couple had had three children but now there were five — two daughters, Mohsina and Shahamine, and three sons, Sheik Mohsin, Shahameen and Shahin. The oldest child was fourteen, the youngest four.

The poverty of the place was obvious and I wondered whether Mumtaz regretted having so many children, so many mouths to feed.

'They have already come to this world,' she said. 'God has given, so what to do? Everybody feels that if the number was smaller it would be good, but what to do now? I had a son after my daughter and I could easily have stopped there, but my husband did not want to and so, for fear of having a conflict, I just kept quiet.'

Nine years earlier her husband had been a landless labourer but he was now working as a lorry driver. He didn't drive long distances but was often away from home for one or even two weeks at a time.

'How much does your husband earn?' I asked.

'He gives me 250 *rupees* when he comes at the weekend,' she said. 'The rest, whatever he is earning, I do not know, but he does buy clothes for the family.'

I had noticed a hen with a few chicks scratching in the dirt outside her hut and asked how many she had now. Two hens, she said, and just a few chicks, but the number fluctuated. Sometimes the chicks were killed by disease and sometimes she sold them off, but with two hens she could soon be up to twenty again. Once a chick had grown she could sell it for about 120 *rupees*.

'Do you usually sell them or eat them?' I asked.

'You can see this is a very poor family,' she said. 'Basically, the chicks are for marketing. I need the money to pay for the children's tuition.'

The children had gathered around her and two of the boys — twelve-year-old Sheik Mohsin and seven-year-old Shahameen — were small and thin for their ages. Mumtaz said that Sheik Mohsin in particular was a sickly boy. He was doing well at school but had hearing problems and sometimes had difficulty breathing. Her own health was also bad. She had an ulcer and often suffered bad headaches. Her sister-in-law had studied tailoring with CSD and was earning extra money by doing embroidery from home for a wholesaler in Calcutta, but Mumtaz said her headaches meant that she couldn't, as she put it, 'make flowers on saris.'

'Have you seen a doctor?' I asked.

'I go to the CSD health centre but I have never approached doctors,' she said. 'If I go to a doctor he will ask for money.'

'What did the CSD workers advise you?'

'To go to a big doctor, but I don't have money so how can I go?'

Her priority, she said, was not her own health but the health of her children. She wanted them to grow up strong, but we could see for ourselves that they weren't.

'Can you tell me what you'll be giving them to eat to-night?' I asked.

'Rice and potatoes,' she said, laughing, 'because they are the cheapest.'

'How often do you eat meat or fish?'

'That's very rare. Maybe once a month.'

I wondered whether Mumtaz had any other means to make money, apart from raising chickens and waiting for her husband to come home.

'I have a lot of family work for the children so I am hardly left with enough time to do any other work,' she said. 'It seems that I need someone to work for me!'

The sun was getting low in the sky and would soon disappear behind the mango trees and so I sug-

gested a break while I took some photographs. Immediately, I was surrounded by children, all smiling and shouting with excitement, trying to squeeze themselves into every shot, but as I played with them I noticed Anirban having a quiet, private

conversation with Mumtaz. Later, he walked over to me.

'She became quite emotional,' he said. 'She said the real problem is her husband's attitude and she told me that she actually does go to work as a domestic helper for three hours every morning. She said, "I have hidden this from our guest."'

The pieces of the jigsaw were beginning to fall into place.

I asked Mumtaz to show me around her home, mainly to get us away from the crowd of relatives and CSD workers who seemed to be intimidating her. She protested that the hut was so old and humble and, in a patronizing attempt to ease her embarrassment, I told her that it was bigger than some flats in Hong Kong and that her children had much more room to play.

'Why don't you stay here then and we'll go there?' said the smiling sister-in-law.

The hut was built of mud with thick walls and a roof which was a bamboo frame covered with heavy clay tiles. Mumtaz said the roof should have been lifted higher above the walls of the hut to improve the ventilation. 'In the summer, the tiles get hot and then because the roof is low the whole room is like a furnace,' she said.

There were three rooms, of which the middle one was the bedroom where Mumtaz and her children slept most nights, three on the bed and three on the floor. When her husband came home, the children slept in the bedroom and she slept with him outside. To one side of the bedroom was a dilapidated storeroom and to the other a very small room in which firewood was stacked for cooking and the chickens were barricaded at night. The kitchen was outside and little more than a shelf of baked mud, under the overhanging tiles of the roof.

The rooms were dark, each having just one window across which had been placed a wooden grill. There were no doors in the hut and the floor was bare earth. Bedding was stored in two sacks in the roof and there was nothing which did not have a clear and useful function. It was the most basic of homes.

Water came from a communal well. Mumtaz said she could no longer manage to carry a full bucket but that there was never a shortage of water. 'The well's very deep and the water is so good,' she said. I noticed that the sister-in-law's hut had electricity — a fan had cooled us as we chatted and one of her sons had been watching a football match on television — but Mumtaz's did not.

However, change was coming. The Indian government had made funds available for the improvement of rural housing and the local *panchayat* had decided to subsidize a new home for Mumtaz. The existing mud hut was twenty years old and liable to be destroyed by termites, so a new brick hut was being built just behind the existing one and would be ready for occupation within a couple of months. The government was paying 13,000 *rupees* towards the cost and Mumtaz was paying another 400. She was taking a close interest in the work. She had asked for a damp course to be added and was paying for it herself at a cost of 80 *rupees*, and had decided to economize by using the tiles from her old hut and to ask the government to use the saving to pay for a concrete lintel. The new hut would not be any bigger than the existing one — in fact, it looked slightly smaller — but it would at least be more durable and Mumtaz hoped one day to have enough money to be able to add one extra room at the back.

She stood back and looked at the new hut, swathed in the shadows of late afternoon.

'I have been married for seventeen long years,' she said, 'but the situation has remained the same since the beginning. It has not improved. Ah, there is so much to say... I thought that perhaps the children would be good, but I see some days when I have to beg for food to cook for them. I have even seen times when my children did not eat for two or three days. Though my relatives help, they are also not landholders, so they can help me only within their capacity. I am worried about when will the situation improve.'

Breaking away from her relatives seemed to have lifted the

pressure on Mumtaz and she began to speak more freely. She even mentioned her husband's attitude.

With a wry smile she said, 'My husband has just been in a good mood and given me two new saris costing 90 *rupees* each.'

She decided to tell me openly about her work as a house-maid, and explained that she worked from seven until ten every morning, seven days a week. Her duties included sweeping, cleaning the house, cleaning the cow shed, fetching water and preparing *masalas*. For this, she was paid 40 *rupees* per month. One dollar. Yes, per month. Twice a year, at festivals, her employer gave her new clothes and every day she was given one meal. She laughed bitterly. 'But the rice they give me — I could eat double.'

I asked Mumtaz what had changed for her since my previous visit.

'I am keeping the same,' she said. 'I don't have much change. I have so many children, my husband's earnings are so small. With that much money, is it possible to look after so many children?'

No, I thought, it isn't.

Mumtaz's answers had been beginning to sound like the whingeing of a woman for whom nothing was ever right, but, come to think of it, nothing much *was* right. In a place of grinding rural poverty, this half-abandoned, illiterate woman was struggling to bring up five children. She alone was holding her family together. Yes, life was a daily struggle and, no, her children were not in the best of health, but they were at least alive, in school and seemingly happy. That was the achievement not of a whinger but of a stoic.

Mohsina, the eldest daughter, came out of the old hut and gave Anirban and me freshly boiled eggs to eat, and then

Mumtaz handed me a present of two small, wrinkled cucumbers, the only produce she had left in her garden. I was embarrassed to accept a gift but, knowing she would be far more embarrassed if I refused, accepted with thanks and humility.

The family budget was so excruciatingly small that I felt I must try to make a contribution, but I didn't want to offend or patronize Mumtaz. Then I had a bright idea.

'Do you have any more eggs for sale?' I said.

Mumtaz laughed and said there were only two and that she would be happy to give them to me. She sent Mohsina back into the house to fetch them.

'No,' interjected Anirban, understanding my intention. 'He insists on paying for them and he will pay the price which he would pay in Hong Kong.'

Mumtaz went into the bedroom to find a plastic bag for the two eggs and, flouting custom and good manners for a moment, I followed her in and handed her 200 *rupees*, which she received with a confused smile and quickly hid in her sari. When I worked as a consultant in Hong Kong I charged the equivalent of 200 *rupees* for one minute's work. For Mumtaz, it was five months' wages.

Earlier in the day I had thought it might be fun to re-enact our chicken counting escapade of nine years earlier, but after seeing how harshly the intervening years had treated Mumtaz I hadn't the heart. It was time to leave.

'Goodbye,' said Mumtaz with a big smile. 'Don't wait ten years before you come again.'

The light was fading as we picked our way back along the path towards the community hall and talked through Mumtaz's story with two village woman who worked for CSD. They said that while Mumtaz had spoken discreetly about her husband's attitude, the truth was that he was well-known for beating her. The women's group in the village had even called a meeting to discuss the case, and the reason why Mumtaz had just received two new saris was that Mr. Sajahan's three brothers had criticized him for his treatment of her.

Dr. Niyogi said that as a lorry driver Mr. Sajahan should be making 2,000 or 3,000 *rupees* per month and so if Mumtaz was receiving only 250 *rupees* once a week — or once a fortnight, or whenever he deigned to come home — he was obviously spending the rest on himself. Also, given that he wasn't driving long distance routes, it was odd that he didn't come home at night and sometimes stayed away for as long as one or two weeks at a time.

'You think there might be another woman?' I asked.

'I should think so,' he said.

Well, perhaps it was wrong to speculate, but Rabeya Bibi and Mumtaz Begum had each started off with 100 *rupees* and each had used the money to buy four chicks. One had flourished, the other had struggled and the reason for the difference in their fortunes seemed to lie in Rabeya's simple, innocent comment, 'My husband is quite helpful.'

I turned back for one last look and there was Mumtaz with her children around her, still standing where we had left them beside the path, waving and smiling as night closed in.

CHAPTER 7

Pakistan, Karachi

Abdul Razzak

First Encounters

'I have to warn you,' said Sister Jeannine, 'that some of our patients are quite badly deformed. If you'd rather not meet them, it's no problem.'

It was a sunny afternoon in the springtime of 1988. I had arrived in Karachi only a couple of hours earlier and knew nothing about leprosy. Just a dim recollection of Sunday school stories in which lepers rang bells wherever they went and shouted 'unclean, unclean.' I had no idea what to expect but had come to Karachi to learn, so our tour of the wards began.

The Marie Adelaide Leprosy Centre (MALC) was in the heart of the old city and in addition to housing an eighty bed hospital was the headquarters of a huge anti-leprosy programme which stretched to the most distant corners of Pakistan. The hospital was not modern and the patients were in small rooms of two or three beds. I remember the steep stone staircases, the cool cream walls, shafts of sunlight slanting through shuttered windows. I remember cradling the hands of patients who had lost their fingers yet yearned for physical contact.

Outside one room, Sister Jeannine stopped.

'Are you okay?' she asked.

I nodded.

'The woman in this next room is very bad. If you don't want to see her, it's okay but you tell me now. Last week one visitor came in here and was so frightened that he ran out. The woman was very much upset.'

'No,' I said, 'I'd like to meet her.'

Zakia was sitting on her bed, swathed in white cotton. She had almost lost her nose and had no fingers. She could not walk. She was almost blind. She could no longer close her eyes and so at night the nurses had to place pads over them to prevent dust blowing in from the street and causing irritation. And she had lost her eyebrows, which may seem a small detail but actually had a horribly dehumanizing effect.

She had come from a village in Afghanistan. As a girl, she had been thrown out of home and locked in a stable. Her family, who loved her but were terrified of her disease, tossed food to her through the stable door. Zakia remained in the stable, leprosy rampaging through her body, until Dr. Ruth Pfau, the intrepid German Sister who was the driving force behind MALC, happened to find her during a trip to Afghanistan and brought her back to Karachi for treatment.

Zakia had first been locked in the stable when she was just six years old. By the time Dr. Pfau rescued her, she was a woman of twenty-six.

Yet she was remarkably cheerful and joked with Sister Jeannine. I sat on her bed and told her about Hong Kong. She taught me how to greet people in Urdu and I taught her a few words of Cantonese. We got on well. I tried to treat her as a woman, not as a collection of disabilities, and feelings of fear or revulsion never crossed my mind.

The next day my introduction to leprosy continued when I went with a young Pakistani medical worker, James Daniel, to a clinic in Malir, on the eastern outskirts of Karachi. Paramedical staff from MALC surveyed families in the area and people suspected of having leprosy were referred to the clinic to be checked by James and his colleagues.

The clinic was already in full swing when a girl walked in, holding a younger boy by the hand. She had come originally from Baluchistan, the vast desert province in the west of Pakistan, and was wearing an exquisite dress, brilliantly coloured and decorated with tiny pieces of glass. She and her brother had been checked by MALC field staff and had come to the clinic for a full professional examination. The girl was ushered behind a curtain to be examined by a woman doctor while her younger brother came and stood beside James's table. I recorded the boy's examination in my diary.

One look at the patch of bright red skin on the boy's cheek confirmed the worst. Leprosy. James took a new file, opened it and wrote, 'Case 2713. Abdul Razzak, son of Abdul Rehman, eight years old.'

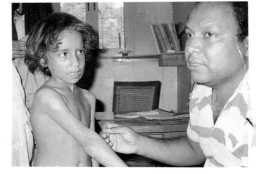

The boy took off his shirt and there were patches on his chest and arms. He took off his trousers to reveal more patches, including a big one on his right

knee. Then James took a pin and told the boy to stretch out his arm and close his eyes. He pricked his arm and the boy winced. Then he told the boy to keep his eyes closed and he pushed the pin into a patch of discoloured skin — and there was no reaction. James pushed the pin in deep — still no reaction. All feeling lost. Leprosy.

Sister Jeannine had warned me that I might find it distressing to meet patients with hideous deformities, but it was this little boy, apparently quite normal, dressed in dirty grey clothes and with his hair tousled, who showed me the tragedy of leprosy. I remembered Zakia and was suddenly very frightened. The boy's body was covered with leprous patches and it seemed unbearably cruel that he too should be facing a life of deformity and rejection. I seemed to be looking at a child whose life was about to fall apart.

And then James put down his pen, told the boy to put his clothes on and turned to me.

'Well,' he said, 'he's lucky. We've caught him just in time. If we had found him three or four months later it would have been very bad, and the deformities would probably have started. It will take a couple of years but we will cure him.'

It was the happiest, most wonderful moment in all my years of working with Oxfam. I wanted to take the little lad in my arms and tell him, 'You don't know how lucky you are.'

James explained that a new method of treatment would stop the spread of the disease within three months and prevent any further risk of contagion. The drugs would turn the boy's skin grey but in time his natural colour would return and the leprous patches would disappear. If he were lucky, he might even regain feeling in the affected areas.

I have told Razzak's story countless times over the years, yet as I sit here writing it now it still brings tears to my eyes. Sometimes it seems like a fairy tale, almost too good to be true.

The Fight against Leprosy

The Marie Adelaide Leprosy Centre (MALC) was born in Karachi in 1956 in a place too terrible to contemplate.

On McLeod Road, near the main railway station, one hundred and fifty leprosy patients lived in a cluster of illegal huts made of bamboo poles, cardboard boxes and straw mats. In the rainy season, the huts were knee-deep in drainage water. The filth was indescribable and the stench appalling. Many of the people had lost all feeling in their hands and feet and at night rats came and gnawed at their limbs. It was a place of utter degradation.

Appalled by the squalor, a few missionary Sisters began to treat the patients from a makeshift clinic. The Sisters had no water or electricity but they did have medical training and, more importantly, they had vocations. They were willing not just to touch the untouchables but to embrace them. Soon patients from all over Karachi flocked to McLeod Road for treatment, and from those humble beginnings MALC grew into a professional, nationwide anti-leprosy programme with more than eight hundred staff. In 1996, due largely to MALC's efforts, leprosy was finally controlled in Pakistan — not eradicated, but brought down below the rate of one active patient per ten thousand people, at which point the World Health Organisation reckoned it ceased to be a public health problem.

Leprosy is a skin disease which also attacks the peripheral

nerves. The first signs are usually small discoloured patches of skin, and unless the disease is treated quickly the patches spread and the patient loses feeling in those areas. Deformities are often caused not *by* leprosy but as a result of it — a smoker with anaesthetized fingers doesn't feel his cigarette burning low, the leprous woman who steps on broken glass feels no pain.

Pakistan's leprosy problem has long been concentrated in Karachi which, with thirteen million inhabitants, is the country's largest city and the place to which migrants have flocked from India, Bangladesh, Afghanistan and less developed parts of Pakistan. Most patients come from poor families, where water is in short supply and many people live together in overcrowded, poorly ventilated rooms, sharing beds and utensils.

Yet, despite those old bible stories and contrary to popular belief, leprosy is far less infectious than flu or a common cold and is contracted only through very close physical contact. MALC staff offered themselves as proof of how little risk the disease poses in most situations.

'I am working here for more than seventeen years,' said one. 'I have worked on the wards. I have taken maggots from the patients' wounds with my own bare hands. Most of the patients here have infectious leprosy, so I should have been the first target but — nothing.'

A vaccine against the disease is not yet generally available, but a powerful treatment is — Multi Drug Therapy (MDT), introduced in 1983. If leprosy is detected early, it can now be completely cured within two years, leaving the patient with no deformities. A patient can even continue to live a normal life while undergoing treatment, although the skin turns grey and the cure does require adherence to a strict timetable. The patient takes daily doses at home, but once every thirty days must receive another single dose under supervision. Missing a month means going back to the start of the two-year cycle and starting again.

Most people who contract leprosy do not need hospital treatment, but when I returned to Karachi in 1997 the eighty beds in MALC's hospital were still full. I stayed in a room beside the hospital and, as I had done ten years before, walked around the wards. The patients this time seemed older. There was a woman who had come from Afghanistan and another from Rajasthan. One old man was dying of cancer, another with a fine white beard had trouble with his kidneys. A few patients were recovering from eye operations and quite a number were horribly deformed.

A young nurse accompanied me into the main female ward. Spotting the camera around my neck, some of the patients immediately covered their faces, but others were happy to talk. Especially Dhasthageer. She was a real character, an old woman sitting in front of a window, wrapped in a white and gold scarf, smiling a toothy smile. She had married at thirteen but been widowed at eighteen and left alone to bring up four children, three of whom had since died. In her old age, she

lived with her one surviving son and five grandchildren.

'She comes in every few months,' said the nurse. 'She has trouble with ulcers on her right hand and foot.'

177

Dhasthageer was tucking into her lunch of rice and *dhal*, but paused for a moment and spoke in Urdu. The nurse smiled.

'What did she say?' I asked.

'She says to tell you that she can still look after herself!' she said.

Not all patients had Dhasthageer's positive attitude.

Bashir Vincent, who led MALC's team of medical social workers, said, 'There's still a stigma to leprosy. First of all, people lose their own sense of worth. They ask, why did I get this leprosy? Maybe I did some sin and that is why. And then, of course, other people begin to discriminate against them. Women feel the discrimination more, particularly if they are deformed. Their husbands can leave them, their in-laws can leave them, but if a man is deformed he can still marry and have children. Our work is really to make people realize that they are still human beings, that they still have their own worth, and we have to do that not just with patients but with their families and communities as well.'

MALC had started a number of projects to enable women who had had leprosy or whose husbands had leprosy to earn money. At Manghopir, north of Karachi, women did sewing and

embroidery, and in Orangi I visited a small but flourishing leather workshop. The thirteen women at Orangi worked a five and a half day week and earned between 1,500 and 2,000 *rupees** per month, producing good quality bags and purses, most of which were sold overseas.

Superstitions and traditional attitudes often frustrated the MALC workers. One told me in exasperation about an infected girl who was refusing to take MDT because her father had told

* US$1 = 50 *rupees*

her it would make her sterile. Bashir Vincent said it was common for people to throw up their hands and say, '*Inshallah*,' it's God's will, instead of trying to overcome their difficulties. While respecting traditional beliefs and cultures, MALC staff tried to encourage social change by, for example, supporting the education of girls or demonstrating cheap ways of improving hygiene.

MALC tried to practise what it preached about the social integration of leprosy patients by employing them whenever possible. It had found jobs for forty-two in Karachi and Sind Province alone, including a delightful man called Muhammed Hussain Sultan.

When Muhammed was a boy of sixteen, living in rural Sind, Dr. Pfau diagnosed his leprosy and brought him to Karachi for treatment. She encouraged him to pass his matriculation exams and after that she offered him a job. For the past twenty-nine years, Muhammed had been working for MALC in various roles, and when I met him he was tucked away in a little room at the back of the building, the man in charge of making shoes for patients.

Many untreated leprosy patients have deformed feet and require special shoes, which have to be stuck together or hand stitched because protruding tacks could  seriously injure a person with an anaesthetized foot. Most Pakistanis wear flat, backless sandals, but Muhammed made them with reinforced soles to prevent ulcers and with backstraps to prevent them slipping off without the wearer's knowledge. He made small boots, taking a plaster cast of each deformed foot and then shaping the boot to match. He made special shoes for patients such as office workers who did not want their colleagues to know that they had leprosy. It was hard work, hand stitching through thick leather and rubber, but Muhammed and one colleague produced hundreds of pairs of sandals and shoes every year.

Karachi had become Muhammed's home. He was married and had two daughters of whom he was enormously proud. He enjoyed his work.

'I make the shoe for the patient and then the ulcer heals. That's very nice. I feel very happy,' he said.

Just around the corner from Muhammed's little workshop  was the hospital pharmacy, run by an old Mexican Sister, Berenice Vargas. Like Dr. Pfau, she had been involved in MALC from the early days in McLeod Road. For forty years, unnoticed and unrecognized, she had done her work, ordering and issuing drugs and training up young pharmacists. One of her former students was now running the pharmacy with her.

I suggested to Sister Vargas that she must feel very proud of MALC's achievements, but she sidestepped the implied praise and talked instead about the wonders of Multi Drug Therapy.

'To see a patient cured and returned to the community, that is a wonderful thing,' she said.

Then she frowned.

'But drugs are getting so expensive these days.'

'How much do the MDT drugs cost?' I asked.

'For one month's treatment now it's about 100 *rupees* per patient,' she said, pulling a long face. 'It used to be just fifty.'

I made the calculation. It was still less than 50 dollars to cure a person completely of a terrible disease.

Beginnings and Endings

Every evening at sunset the rooftop of the Marie Adelaide Leprosy Centre provided the most spectacular view. As the sun sank into the Arabian Sea, hundreds of kites wafted in wide circles across the sky, their outstretched wings catching the last of the golden light. I watched them night after night, entranced by the ease with which they soared above the heaving city, circling higher and higher until they were mere specks against the darkening sky.

Down in the streets, Karachi was charmless — flat, grey, dirty, dusty and smelly. The people were, without exception, friendly, courteous and hospitable, but I couldn't feel at ease on streets where men outnumbered women by one hundred to one. It was not so much the absence of women which unsettled me as the superfluity of men. The place was too masculine.

One morning I set off with a driver, heading north from the city centre, bound for Manghopir. Good roads ran through affluent suburbs, but then we turned off onto rougher tracks and began to head towards a huge cement works. It was a scorching hot day and the buses and carts scuffed up billowing

clouds of dust which covered the bushes in ghostly, mourning grey. Brightly coloured trucks lumbered past us, stacked high with stone, and in each small roadside town

181

stores were selling building blocks, concrete pipes and slabs of marble. Many of the people were from Afghanistan, families who had fled the fighting in their own country and now worked as stone breakers. They were easy to spot, lacking the darkness of the Pakistanis. Some of the Afghan children, particularly the girls, were extraordinarily beautiful, with dreamy grey eyes and hair the colour of rope.

I was going to visit a school for the children of leprosy patients and the children of people who worked at Manghopir leprosy hospital. I had been to the same spot ten years before and remembered a patch of scruffy land in the middle of nowhere and an enthusiastic Sister explaining why Oxfam Hong Kong should pay for a kindergarten and primary school to be built there. We eventually approved a grant and in due course received photographs of the completed building, but I certainly wasn't expecting the large compound which suddenly appeared before us now, all freshly painted and glimmering in the sunlight like a palace in the desert.

The school had started as a kindergarten and primary school but after a few years had been extended to include an afternoon secondary section. New classrooms and a laboratory had been added and a hostel for seventy teenaged girls had been built nearby. The whole compound was run by the Daughters of the Heart of Mary, and Sister Catherine, one of the five Pakistani Sisters in the order and herself a qualified teacher, showed me around.

There were 649 children enrolled in the school's three sections and almost all were from very poor families. In the kindergarten, for example, threequarters of the children's families were too poor to pay the monthly fee of 110 *rupees*. Families were hazy about the ages at which their children should begin the various stages of education. Kindergarten children could be anything from four to eight years old and some students didn't finish secondary studies until they were twenty-five.

The quality of education provided by the secondary school did not seem high. Forty-seven children had taken their matriculation exams the previous year but only twenty-one had passed, whereas at another school run by the Sisters fifty-four of fifty-seven had passed. The difference seemed to be that the second school had a qualified principal, whereas at Manghopir a Sister tried to combine the duties of being a principal with one hundred and one other responsibilities. One senior teacher hadn't been seen or heard of for two months!

The kindergarten was run on typically Asian lines, drilling knowledge into the children so that they would pass an exam and be able to move on to primary school. I joined what the teacher said was a maths class but was really no more than recognition of numbers. Each child in turn was called to the front of the class and given a cane with which to point to the numbers in ascending order, while their classmates chanted them in Urdu. It was extraordinarily repetitive, starting each time at 0 and working up to 20. Some of the children were so small that, even standing on tiptoes and stretching out the cane, they could barely reach the higher numbers.

'Do they do any art or handicrafts or learning through play?' I asked Sister Catherine.

'Not much,' she said, 'because they have a syllabus to finish.' She emptied one child's bag to show me a pile of textbooks, and explained that the children had to sit three papers in Urdu, English and maths, as well as taking an oral test.

'How much English do they have to know to pass a paper in it?' I asked.

Sister Catherine laughed.

'Just a few words,' she said. 'Good morning, good afternoon, how are you, I am fine, thank you.'

It might not seem much, but for these children English was a third language. At home with their families they spoke Persian, Pashto, Baluchi or Punjabi, and before thinking about English had first to get to grips with the national language, Urdu.

Visits to kindergartens and primary schools are always happy because the children are so eager to learn. They have so much life in front of them. But just five minutes' walk from the school was MALC's Home for the Handicapped, a place for people who had most of their lives behind them.

Daniel Karamat, the man in charge, led us into the dining room, where the residents were having lunch. There were almost forty of them, mostly old, many from Afghanistan. All had suffered from leprosy and many had serious disabilities and deformities. A couple had had legs amputated, some were blind, others had horribly mutilated faces. I had thought I might find Zakia living here but couldn't see her.

'Do the patients have families who come to visit them?' I asked.

'No, most of them are alone for many years,' said Daniel. 'Nobody comes to see them. It's very sad.'

'What do they do all day?'

'Well, those who can still walk are paid to act as cleaners around the place. A few go to school to learn writing and reading. Some work as gardeners or fetch the bread. A few work as *chowkidars* or watchmen.' He laughed. 'Actually, we have nothing to watch, but it's just to keep them busy, you can say.'

'What happens when a patient dies? Do the others get very depressed?'

'No,' said Daniel. 'Actually, in the last six months eleven patients died. Most of them were very old and the other patients didn't feel bad because — well, it's part of the game, you can say! There was one old man who was very sick, out of his mind, messing up his bed and all. Really, the residents thanked God when he went up.'

Went up. A nice way of putting it.

We left the dining room and Daniel led us upstairs and along a corridor to a balcony framed by branches of vivid pink bougainvillea. There, on the cool stone floor, sat a woman, having her lunch alone.

Zakia.

I wish I could say that her life had improved since our first meeting in the hospital ten years earlier, that she had finally found peace, that her story had a happy ending, but it was not so. Quite the reverse.

Many people had tried to help Zakia. The doctors had brought her some early relief with an operation which allowed her to close her eyes. Reconstructive surgery had improved her face and special shoes had allowed her to get around the hospital. But the mental and emotional trauma of being isolated and rejected for all those years had taken its toll and she had become seriously disturbed, prone to bouts of dark despair and bursts of furious, violent anger. Fresh wounds on her face showed how she sometimes turned her anger on herself. She had her own room and Daniel had even hired an Afghan woman to be with her twenty-four hours a day, conversing with her in her native Persian, but much of what Zakia said was incomprehensible, the mutterings of a wounded mind. So many people had done so much, but it was all too late.

'What a life,' I said quietly to Sister Catherine.

'Misery,' she said. 'Really, misery.'

A nagging professional voice in my head said, 'Go on, take a photo. People will want to see what she looks like.' Well, I'm sorry, but I couldn't do it. I couldn't take a photo and I won't try to paint a picture in words. I have a picture in my mind but that is where it will stay, too sad for sharing.

Ten years earlier when we had met at the hospital, there had been a sense of hope, a feeling that she might yet be able to salvage something from the ruins of her childhood. This time there was no hope. She was fading, physically and mentally.

The end will come, and when it does I will thank God that Zakia too has finally gone up. May she find peace at last.

'A Normal Student'

Sometimes you get lucky, and the day we went looking for Abdul Razzak was one of those days.

The previous evening I had spoken to James Daniel, the man who had diagnosed Razzak's leprosy ten years earlier. He was a short, stocky, cheerful man who, like his father before him, had devoted his life to fighting leprosy, joining the centre back in the days when most people wouldn't go near the place for fear of infection. I explained what I was trying to do and produced an old picture of him examining Razzak. He had a good look at it, flicking through his mental records, trying to recall one face among many thousands. We agreed that the first step would be to go back to the Malir clinic and try to find Razzak's address.

But the next morning James greeted me with a broad grin.

'I've been doing some thinking,' he said. 'At first I thought the boy was Indian but then I remembered his mother. His sister was also a patient, wasn't she?'

'Yes,' I said. 'She brought him to the clinic.'

'*Achaa*, so I know the address because we used their home to distribute medicines to other patients in that area. We can go straight there, no need to go the clinic. I can remember.'

Then he added, 'His case number was 2714, or something like that. Right?'

2713. What a memory!

We climbed into a small, battered white van and set off into the morning traffic. Our driver, Allahbuksh, had a wonderful face, all smile and silver stubble, and, like so many of the staff, had worked at MALC for donkey's years.

Now he nudged his way between elaborately decorated buses, donkey carts, lorries belching black smoke and little motorized tricycles that buzzed around us like flies. As Allahbuksh hooted

at all and sundry and weaved his way through impossibly small gaps in the traffic, James explained that treating leprosy in Pakistan was not simply a medical matter.

'We're not treating patients,' he said. 'If we look at people as patients, we'll never build up that relationship, that trust, which we need. We're all like one family, like a team, jointly implementing the programme.'

The patient, he said, had to trust the medical worker and together with the family had to ensure that the drugs were taken regularly. In turn, the medical worker had to understand the patient's social and financial situation and try to help with any difficulties.

We had been travelling for about half an hour, heading east out of Karachi, when James suddenly shouted to Allahbuksh to stop. He jumped out of the van and ran back along the road. I thought he had gone to check whether we had missed a turning, but in fact he had spotted a woman he knew. As he ran towards her, she thought he was going to attack her and froze in fear, but then she recognized him and laughed.

'Jimmy, Jimmy,' she said.

He introduced me and explained what I was doing. The woman kissed my hand in welcome.

'This is Razzak's mother,' said James, who had now become Jimmy. 'I thought I recognized her.'

One face in a crowd passed at speed, a face last seen eight years earlier. The man's memory and powers of observation were extraordinary.

Razzak's mother was dressed in a vivid orange *shalwar-qamiz*, the traditional long, loose-fitting shirt worn over baggy trousers, with a purple scarf covering her head and shoulders. She wore her greying hair in a thick pigtail and had a stud through one side of her nose. She was blind in one eye, the result of a childhood injury.

She joined us in the van and we rode the short distance to her home, turning off the main road and bumping slowly along rough, narrow tracks that wound their way between the walls of single-storey brick homes. Occasionally, the van splashed through a puddle of stagnant water or slowed while a kid goat skittered out of the way. Little dust storms whipped up the plastic bags and paper scraps that littered the lanes.

Allahbuksh stopped beside a long cream wall and Razzak's mother ushered us through an iron gate which was covered by a curtain of old sacks. We stepped into the family compound. There were three single-room houses in a straight line, each with its back to the exterior wall and with a verandah in front. In front of all three houses was an area of bare earth, swept immaculately clean, where a couple of chickens scratched around and two large tethered goats chewed at a pile of grass. A pile of tin plates and cooking pots was waiting to be washed.

We were led into one of the three houses, which was actually a single room with a high ceiling and one window. The only furniture was a double bed, on which we sat, a television and a cabinet containing the family's more precious possessions — sets of crockery and bars of soap. Along one wall ran a high shelf, on which were displayed decorated enamel trays and more sets of cups and saucers.

As Razzak's mother slipped away to make tea, so his father appeared. The head of the family. He was dressed in a pale blue *shalwar-qamiz* and walked slowly and with difficulty, using a stick. We shook hands and he asked if we would like to drink cold water. We explained that tea was already being prepared.

'You come to my house. Why do you not drink cold water?' he asked.

So we drank cold water. We also drank tea, and Jimmy asked father about his left leg. The old man sat on the floor and explained the problem in Urdu and in great detail.

'It's a type of eczema,' Jimmy summarized. 'I've told him to come to the centre next week and we'll see what to do.'

The warmth of the relationship between Jimmy and the family was remarkable, particularly as they had not seen him for more than eight years. They were so comfortable in his company that the traditional restrictions of *purdah* were relaxed and

daughters, daughters-in-law and hordes of young children emerged from the other houses and began to fill the room, sitting on the floor or standing shyly in the doorway. As the conversation flowed, the women contributed their ideas and information and Razzak's mother spoke freely and even agreed to pose for a photograph, but everyone deferred to the old man. He might have been squatting on the floor with a gammy leg, but he was still the patriarch.

Among the women who had slipped silently into the room was Husni, Razzak's elder sister who had brought him to the clinic ten years earlier and who had herself been treated for two years. Jimmy examined her chin and found no trace of leprosy. Indeed, she was a lovely-looking young woman with a charming, fresh smile.

I looked at the large family sitting around us and realized there was only one person missing. The one whom we had come to meet — Razzak. He, we were told, was at school.

Father's name was Rehman and mother was called Amina and when I asked how old they were it sparked off a debate to which every family member seemed to contribute an estimate. Some said fifty, others said sixty and son Rafiq went as high as seventy.

'Sixty to seventy, it's okay,' said Jimmy, tilting his head, obviously bemused by this strange Western preoccupation with times and dates. They were as old as they were.

Rehman and Amina had eleven children, six sons and five daughters, ranging in age from thirty-five down to fourteen. Three of the daughters had married and gone to live with their husbands, but the rest of the family lived in the compound, including the wives of the first three sons and a growing band of grandchildren.

'How many grandchildren do you have altogether?' I asked.

'Well, eldest daughter has five daughters and two sons, and second daughter has five sons and three daughters, and third daughter has three sons and five daughters and eldest son...'

The conclusion was that the tally so far was twenty-nine,

but of course that was with only half the children married and some of them only just getting into the swing of parenthood. When all eleven children were up to full production the total would climb into the sixties or seventies — and the eldest grandson was already twenty and eminently marriageable. It seemed likely that before they died Rehman and Amina would have more than one hundred direct descendants.

Rehman had been born in the compound where we sat, but his parents had come from Baluchistan. They were Brahui people from an area northwest of Karachi, towards the border with Afghanistan.

Rehman remembered as a boy in Malir being able to look across fields to the distant railway line, where trains ran to and from Karachi, but that view had long since been obscured by densely packed houses and a busy highway. Rehman seemed to reckon that most of the changes he had seen in his lifetime had been for the worse.

'In those days,' he said, 'people were very healthy. No head-aches or stomach pains. There were few doctors but no complaints.'

He shook his head and looked down at the floor.

'The food is not so good now. On the vegetables now they are using gutter water but then they were using fresh water.'

Jimmy added, 'On the road you have seen that the gutters are all open.' Yes, I understood the implications of what the old man was saying.

'Muslims and Hindus were all living here like brothers then,' said Rehman. 'But now...' He paused and looked out of the window. His family looked at him, expectantly. 'Hindus and Muslims used to pay respect to each other, but now even the various Muslims are not living together so well.'

A few years earlier the tensions between rival Muslim factions had been so serious that this section of Malir had been sealed off by police. On a good day, said Rehman, he had seen four or five bodies lying in the lanes but on a bad day he had spotted as many as twelve. Even today there were robberies and the night before our visit a man had been killed. Rehman's family mixed only with other people from Baluchistan, kept themselves to themselves and rarely ventured out at night.

Yet while factional rivalries and political uncertainties were always at the back of the mind, the family's main daily concern was poverty. Rehman put it succinctly. 'If we do for our clothes,' he said, 'we have no food. If we do something for our food, we have no clothes.'

Before his leg started playing up, Rehman had worked as a gardener. Amina was still working as a school cleaner, earning 900 *rupees* per month — less than 20 dollars. One son, Rafiq, worked in a garment factory and the eldest worked in a steel mill. Another loaded cattle on and off trucks for 50 or 60 *rupees* per day and yet another ran a donkey cart. All these were casual jobs with no guarantees of regular income. None of the sons earned more than 2,000 *rupees* per month and three of them had children of their own to clothe and feed. Amina said that when Rehman had gone into hospital for treatment to his leg, she had sold her gold and used her last *rupee* of savings to pay the bill.

Two years ago, when the family budget had been even tighter than normal, Razzak had stopped school for two years in order to save money, but now he was back in class and we decided it was time to go to see him. We finished small cups of sweet milky tea and stood up to leave. A crowd of children followed us out to the van and two of Razzak's cousins came with us to show us the way to the school.

We bumped along a few more dusty lanes, with Jimmy pointing out the houses of other former patients. We passed a cattle market with some pretty sorry-looking cattle, and then just as the school building came into view, one of the cousins shouted to Allahbuksh and we lurched to a halt. In an uncanny repeat of Jimmy's earlier experience, the cousin had spotted Razzak at a roadside stall and called him over.

He was a tall, slim boy, dressed in an orange *shalwar-qamiz*, and obviously had no idea who we were or what we wanted. Jimmy showed him a cutting from an old Oxfam Hong Kong newsletter, in which there was a photograph of the original consultation. Razzak looked at it carefully and pointed to himself in the photo.

'Is that my sister?' he asked.

We all laughed. All except Razzak, who was embarrassed by his mistake.

We got out of the van and walked over to the school, a U-shaped collection of newly built, single-storey classrooms on a small, dusty piece of land. Some four hundred boys studied here, ranging in ages from eleven to eighteen, and almost all of them were, like Razzak, from the Baluchi community.

Jimmy and I went to pay our respects to the headmaster, Samuel Joseph, who told us that the school had moved to the site less than six months earlier, having previously been in an area plagued by factional unrest. The attendance rate had been low and falling, but since the move the percentage of boys attending each day was up to between seventy-five and eighty. However, the new buildings had fallen victim to political changes at national level. They had been started under the People's Works Programme of Benazir Bhutto's government and, when she was defeated, all funds for the programme were stopped. So the buildings remained unfinished, lacking electricity and even a boundary wall. Like so many buildings in Karachi, they looked as though the builders had simply walked away one evening and never returned.

The school worked from seven-thirty in the morning until one o'clock, six days a week, with a holiday on Sunday and an early finish on Friday for weekly prayers at the mosque. There was no entrance examination and the annual fee was only 150 *rupees*, but boys sometimes dropped out for a year or two because their parents could not afford books and uniform. After matriculation, they could go on to further education, although most came under pressure from their families to get a job and start earning.

'We have had people who have gone on from this school to be doctors,' Mr. Joseph said proudly.

'But most of them?' I asked.

'*Achaa*,' he said, tilting his head. 'Most of them will go into agriculture.'

They might become manual workers but they would be able to speak three languages. The school's medium of instruction was Sindhi, the boys learned the national language of Urdu and within their families spoke Baluchi. They even learned English as a foreign language. In most English-speaking countries, such linguistic accomplishments would be regarded as remarkable.

Razzak was in Class Seven and his next lesson was Sindhi, so I went and sat in. The teacher was a tall young man with a booming voice, who told me later that in the evenings he worked as a hospital receptionist, in order to earn an extra 1,500 *rupees* to support his family. The walls of the classroom were unplastered breeze-block and the floor was bare earth. The room had no

lights, no glass in the window and no door in the doorway. Every few minutes a cloud of dust blew through. Twenty-eight boys sat at simple wooden benches, two or three together, sharing textbooks. All wore the uniform orange *shalwar-qamiz* and most were much younger than Razzak.

The teacher read out a passage which the boys followed in their text books, and then called on individual boys to stand up and read aloud. When it was Razzak's turn, he seemed embarrassed and read hesitantly, interrupted a number of times by corrections from the teacher.

After the class, I suggested to the teacher that Razzak had not read well.

'You are one hundred per cent correct,' he said. 'He is a normal student. We have many outstanding students in this school, but he is just normal.'

I hoped to talk to Razzak quietly after school, but he and I were called out of class and taken to the headmaster's study. Razzak must have been terrified, surrounded by the headmaster, the headmaster's clerk, a senior teacher, Jimmy Daniel and this most improbable foreigner. He had inherited a strong nose from his parents and in a few years' time would be a fine-looking man, but for now he was an uneasy, gawky teenager, ready for his first shave, muttering almost inaudible answers to my questions, averting his eyes, picking at his spots. I noticed that his teeth were already stained red from chewing betel.

'Please,' said Mr. Joseph, gesturing towards Razzak. 'You can ask him questions now.'

Well, did Razzak feel uncomfortable, I wondered, studying in a class in which most of the other boys were much younger than him?

Jimmy repeated the question in Urdu and then the teacher repeated it in Baluchi. We all looked at Razzak and waited for his answer.

'I don't feel anything,' he said.

'There are other students like him who are much older than their classmates so this is not a problem,' said Mr. Joseph briskly.

What about when he was being treated for leprosy? Had there been any disruption to his education then? Had he felt isolated?

Jimmy repeated the question in Urdu and the teacher repeated it in Baluchi. Again, we all turned to Razzak. He looked away, pressed his palm to his forehead.

'I didn't feel anything,' he said.

'That would not be a problem,' said Mr. Joseph. 'Baluchi people are very good at accepting people with leprosy. They don't feel any hatred towards a patient.'

This was turning into an interview of the headmaster.

Then a bell rang deliverance. Being Friday, school ended at eleven-thirty to allow the students to attend weekly prayers, and so our stilted conversation was over. Boys came tumbling out of every classroom, a sea of orange cotton swirling in the strong breeze, and, for the first time, Razzak looked at me and smiled.

I suggested that Jimmy and I talk to him later in the privacy of his own home.

'Yes, we go together in the van,' said Jimmy.

We thanked the headmaster, said our goodbyes and shook many hands. A few boys had gathered around a vendor selling soft drinks from a barrow and they wanted their pictures taken. The Sindhi teacher kicked his scooter into life and headed off to his second job. We climbed into the van — only to realize that we had lost Razzak.

So we all got out again, while Jimmy and the cousins asked the last few students whether they had seen him. 'Oh, yes,' they said, 'we saw him. He ran off that way' — and they pointed in the opposite direction to Razzak's home.

Jimmy burst out laughing. 'He was just like this before,' he said. 'Every time I would come to his house he ran away because he thought I would give him injection!'

We decided to return to the house anyway and drove slowly along the lanes, Razzak's cousins keeping their eyes peeled, but we reached the house without seeing any sign of him.

'He'll be back soon,' said his brother Rafiq, surprised to see us again.

'I don't think so,' said Jimmy. 'Certainly not if he sees our van parked here.'

We parted the sacks across the gateway and stepped back into the compound. The sun was now high in the sky and Rehman was sitting on a *charpoi* or rope bed, in the shade of a sprawling crimson bougainvillea, with sundry women, children and grandchildren standing or sitting around him.

Rafiq led us back into the house and we sat again on the double bed. The television was turned on, blaring out Hindi music videos from India. Rehman came and sat on the floor in front of us. Grandchildren gathered in the doorway, and two or three women joined us, one feeding a baby. When fifteen people had taken their places on the floor I stopped counting.

We were all waiting for Razzak.

'What to do?' wondered Jimmy.

'Wait,' I said. A search party of cousins had been despatched to find him.

Eventually, after perhaps half an hour, the cousins returned with Razzak. He did not look exactly delighted to see us. More like a prisoner who knew there was more torture to come. Words were exchanged with the family and with Jimmy.

'Did he really run away from us?' I asked.

'He says No — but I think Yes!' said Jimmy.

Razzak sat on the floor, between Jimmy and his father. He clearly felt easier here than he had in the intimidating presence of the headmaster, but was still not happy to be the focus of everyone's attention. A typically embarrassed teenager.

I asked whether he had enjoyed working as a motor mechanic during the years when he was out of school.

'It's good,' he said. 'But better to go to school.'

What did he want to do when he left school after matriculation?

'Dispenser,' he said.

'Why?'

'I want more information about diseases.'

'Why? Because you suffered from a serious disease yourself?'

'No.'

'Why, then?'

'Personal interest.'

Jimmy joked, 'Because he received such good service himself! That's why he wants to give service.'

Then father spoke.

'It depends on whether we have the money. If we can pay, he will continue his study. I know one fellow who continued studying and is now a doctor. But I am not working, so this is a problem. In college, the fees are higher and he would have to buy books. So if we cannot pay, he will have to work.'

That was that. Father had spoken.

I turned to Rafiq, who was sitting beside me on the bed. He spoke some English, had passed his matriculation and seemed bright. He had already told me that he was not satisfied making jeans and shorts in a garment factory.

'Do you think you might study further and be able to change your job?' I asked.

He laughed. 'I have a child. I have to earn for my children. How can I go for study?'

Evidently, a silly question.

Rafiq's was a 'love marriage' but most marriages were arranged by the parents. Amina said young people usually married 'from fifteen or sixteen and certainly not more than twenty.' Razzak was eighteen. He looked like a boy but was only two years from his mother's deadline. Had he thought about that?

He smiled shyly and looked away. Father answered.

'Nothing has been arranged. First he has to complete his study. Then we will think about marriage.'

Already, nineteen people lived in the three rooms of the compound and the number was growing steadily. I wondered whether there was any possibility that Razzak and his bride might live on their own.

Father dismissed the idea. 'Of course, we will all stay together,' he said.

I began to see how naive I had been in thinking that I

could talk to Razzak and learn about his opinions and aspirations. In a traditional Brahui household, a teenaged son did not have opinions and aspirations. Certainly not while in the company of his father or his headmaster. He did as he was told.

Later, alone with Jimmy and me, Razzak did say that he liked football very much and played every evening with his friends, all of whom were Brahuis like himself or Baluchis. His school team was one of the best in the area and he hoped to be selected for it. Most Baluchi boys, he said, liked football.

'But what about cricket?' I asked. 'I thought Pakistani men were fanatical about cricket.'

'I don't like it,' said Razzak.

Jimmy smiled and said, 'He doesn't give you many words, does he?'

That was true. But his next short answer gave me plenty to think about.

As a small boy, Razzak had been under constant treatment for leprosy for two years. He had had to take drugs every day and once every thirty days Jimmy had come to his home and given him an extra dose. The routine of the treatment had been rigorous and, as Razzak's skin had turned grey, people had been able to tell that he had leprosy. I wondered how much of a scar the whole experience had left on him.

Jimmy translated the question.

Razzak looked at me.

'*Bhool gaya,*' he said. Forgotten.

Jimmy rolled up Razzak's sleeve and held his outstretched arm in an unwitting re-enactment of the original consultation ten years earlier. He checked the same patch of skin, but this time there was no mark. No leprosy. Full feeling had returned. Razzak had been completely cured.

So it was not a fairy tale, not too good to be true. Rather, it was the clearest, most convincing example of medical progress — irrefutable, wonderful progress.

Of course, Razzak remained one of eleven children in a very poor family in a poor quarter of Karachi. His bright young nephew had completed his matriculation by the age of sixteen but even he wasn't being allowed to go on to college, so Razzak's chances of being able to continue his studies seemed slim. Life would remain tough.

But it could have been so much worse. Leprosy doesn't cause death but it does ruin life, disfiguring and deforming the body, caging and wounding the spirit. It happened to Zakia, poor woman, and, if the MALC field workers hadn't found him, it could have happened to Razzak.

Instead, he would have as much chance at life as his brothers. Far from being a daily curse, leprosy for Razzak was not even a distant memory. He would find a job and marry. He would bring his bride back to the family compound to live with his ageing parents and his brothers, and would watch his own children grow.

He would live the life he was born to live.

Reflection

Flowers Coming into Bloom

So the searches which began in Negros with the sadness of one girl's death ended in Karachi with the miracle of one boy's life. Leilani Flores, shrivelled by malnutrition, had been almost forgotten, but Abdul Razzak, who ten years earlier had been ravaged by a terrible disease, was fit and strong and moving into manhood.

Only after leaving Negros did it dawn on me that in one of the island's graveyards, in the fragrant shade of a *calachuchi* tree, there was probably a small grave with a cross or a headstone recording Leilani's brief life. I could have asked her relatives where it was, gone to see it and paid my respects, closed the chapter once and for all, but the thought hadn't even crossed my mind. It had seemed more important to spend time with Leilani's cousins and to learn about their lives.

The past was past. *Bhool gaya*. Forgotten. What mattered now was the present.

Enrique and Bellia Maglantay had somehow managed to scrimp and save enough money to send their eldest daughter to college and still hoped to do the same for Archie and Junryl. In Hong Kong, Ho Yun Chiu had, in his quietly determined way, built a new life for himself as a happy husband, proud father and international sportsman. In his student days, Wittaya Buitsak had written that, 'Children everywhere are like flowers which are just coming into bloom,' and now as a father he was helping his own son to grow strong. Life had dealt Mumtaz Begum a desperate hand, but she struggled on, just about managing to feed and clothe and educate her children, a tough, tenacious, admirable woman. In Calcutta, Nizam, Dheeraj and the other boys were planning their futures, daring to dream. Konda was holding down a good job and talking of how he would make his own children 'every time happy.' And Santosh was chasing dragonflies.

Everything wasn't perfect but most things were better than they had been.

In brilliant sunshine, the plane from Karachi lumbered into the sky and headed east, out over the deserts of Rajasthan.

Contacts

If you would like to support any of the agencies mentioned in this book, or if you would like more information about their work, you can contact them directly at the following addresses.

Oxfam Hong Kong
9/F Breakthrough Centre
191 Woosung Street, Kowloon
Hong Kong, China
Tel   +852 2520 2525
Fax +852 2789 9545
Email info@oxfam.org.hk

**Paediatrics Department
Corazon Locsin Montelibano
Memorial Regional Hospital**
Bacolod, Negros Occidental
Philippines

**Hong Kong Sports Association
for the Physically Disabled**
Unit 141-148, G/F, Block B
Mei Fung House, Mei Lam Estate
Shatin, New Territories
Hong Kong, China
Tel   +852 2602 8232
Fax +852 2603 0106
Email hksap@chevalier.net
http://www.cmsweb.com/hksap/

Duang Prateep Foundation
Lock 6, Art Narong Road
Klongtoey, Bangkok 10110
Thailand
Tel   +66 2 249 3553
Fax +66 2 249 5254
Email dpf@internet.ksc.net.th
http://www.capcat.ksc.net/org/
duang.htm

Future Hope India

6C Surya

52/D Ballygunge Circular Road

Calcutta 700019, West Bengal

India

Tel +91 33 476 9349

Tel/Fax +91 33 475 3676

**Future Hope Hong Kong
Charitable Foundation**

c/o HSBC International Trustees

GPO Box 2247

Hong Kong, China

Tel +852 2822 3744

Fax +852 2877 2959

Future Hope (UK)

6 Queensdale Place

London W11 4SQ

England

Tel/Fax +44 171 371 1769

Centre for Social Development

68 Barrack Road, Barrackpore

24 Parganas (N) 743101

West Bengal, India

Tel +91 33 560 1750

Fax +91 33 560 3172

Marie Adelaide Leprosy Centre

Mariam Manzil

AM 21 Off Shahrah-e-Liaquat

(Frere Road)

PO Box 8666, Karachi 74400

Pakistan

Tel +92 21 568 4151/ 568 2706

Fax +92 21 568 3106

Email malcnlcp@cyber.net.pk

Design and Photographs

This book was designed by John Au.

The following people and agencies supplied photographs: Enrique Maglantay (page 34), Emmanuel Arenas (back cover and page 40), Oriental Daily Press (page 56), Ho Yun Chiu (pages 65 and 66 upper), Duang Prateep Foundation (page 101), Wittaya Buitsak (page 104), Future Hope (pages 116, 135 and 210) and the Centre for Social Development (pages 152 lower, 153, 156 upper and 164).

All other photographs were taken by the author.

The colourful paintings at the front and back of the book are by Manish of Future Hope.

Thanks

This book belongs to the people whose lives it describes and to the many other people mentioned in the text who helped in so many ways. I am grateful to all of them and proud to count them as friends.

Others, whose names do not appear in the text, also gave invaluable help. It was wonderful to work again with John Au, whose professional flair and finesse combine with his personal warmth and understanding to make him the ideal designer. My old comrade Tim Nutt once again provided enormous encouragement and support, as well as generous hospitality. Jeremy Early and Leila Waddington offered sensitive and constructive criticism.

I was also helped by Mary Bale, Randal Bale, Sarah Barnes, Seriphap Chainetn, Stanley Chan, Dr. Thomas Chiang, the team at Chinese University Press, Marie Lisa Dacanay, Jean Dimacali, staff of Duang Prateep Foundation, everyone at Future Hope, Edgar Gonsalves, Malinee Kiatbanlue, S. S. Krishnan, John Kwok, Cristina Lapres, Corie Concordia Law, Doris Lau, Anne Luxmore, Nanette McClintock, Peter Moss, Buck Ng Ting Kin, Hieu Van Ngo, Simone Nutt, Valeria Nutt, staff of Oxfam Hong Kong, staff of PAP 21, Royal Thai Consulate General–Hong Kong, Rubylenne de Paula, Jose 'Ninoy' Pido, Susan Ribeiro, Iain Simpson, UNHCR–Hong Kong, Jamie Walls, Chrissie Webb, Julie Weston, Amphan Wongsawa and Billy Yip. My thanks to all of them.

About the Author

Chris Bale has lived and worked in Hong Kong for twenty years. From 1984 to 1991 he was Director of Oxfam Hong Kong, raising funds to help victims of famine in Ethiopia and Sudan and developing a programme of grants to help poor communities throughout Asia.

He co-founded the Methodist Study Trust to help students with physical disabilities and was Chairman of Trailwalker, Hong Kong's largest charitable sporting event.

In addition to his work with charities, he was for many years the Senior News Presenter for Asia Television's World Channel and produced a number of award winning documentary films. In partnership with Tim Nutt, he wrote *The MacLehose Trail* and *Hong Kong — A Moment In Time*, both published by The Chinese University Press.

In 1986 he was selected as one of Hong Kong's Ten Outstanding Young People and in 1996 was awarded the MBE for services to charity.

He is now based in London as Director General of Befrienders International, the umbrella organization for the Samaritans movement worldwide.